Aq...

Aquarius 1986

Teri King's complete horoscope
for all those whose birthdays fall between
20 January and 19 February

Pan Astral
London and Sydney

Pan Astral regrets that it cannot enter into
any correspondence with readers requesting
information about their horoscope

First published 1985 by Pan Books Ltd,
Cavaye Place, London, SW10 9PG
© Teri King 1985
ISBN 0 330 28761 3

Printed and bound in Great Britain by
Hunt Barnard Printing Ltd, Aylesbury, Bucks

This book is sold subject to the condition that it
shall not, by way of trade or otherwise, be lent, re-sold,
hired out, or otherwise circulated without the publisher's prior
consent in any form of binding or cover other than that in which
it is published and without a similar condition including this
condition being imposed on the subsequent purchaser

Contents

Introduction	7
General Analysis – Positive characteristics	10
Negative characteristics	11
Partnerships	12
Romantic Prospects 1986	22
Health Year 1986	24
Marriage Year 1986	26
Pluto and Your Social Energy	28
Neptune – Your Ideals and Charm	33
Punters' Luck for 1986	39
Your Pets and Astrology	43
The Year in Focus	49
Day-by-day Horoscope	57
The Moon and Your Moods	88

Introduction

Astrology is a very complex science. Whilst it can be useful in assessing the different aspects of human relationships, there are many misconceptions associated with it. Not the least of these is the cynic's question: 'How can zodiac forecasts be accurate for all the millions of people born under any one sign?' The answer is that all horoscopes published in newspapers, books and magazines are, of necessity, of a general nature. Unless an astrologer can work from the date, time and place of your birth, the reading given will only be true to the broadly typical member of your sign.

Take a person born on 1 May. This person is principally a subject of Taurus, simply because the Sun, ruler of willpower and feelings, occupies that portion of the heavens known as Taurus during the period 21 April to 21 May. However, there are other influences to be taken into account, for instance the Moon: this planet, ruler of the subconscious, enters a fresh sign every forty-eight hours. On the birth date in question it may have been in, say, Virgo – and if that were the case it would make this particular subject a Taurean/Virgoan. Then again the rising sign or Ascendant must also be taken into consideration. This also changes constantly, as approximately every two hours a new sign passes over the horizon. The rising sign is of utmost importance, determining the image projected by the subject to the outside world – in effect, the personality. (This is why the time of birth is essential for compiling a natal chart). Let us suppose that in this particular instance Taurus was rising at the time of birth; this would make the individual a Taurean/Virgoan/Taurean. Now, because two of the three main influences are Taurus, the subject would be a fairly typical Taurean, displaying the faults and attributes associated with this sign. But if the Moon and the Ascendant were, say in Aquarius, the subject would portray more the vices and virtues of a true Aquarian.

Throughout the nine planets this procedure is carried on, each making up a significant part of the subject's character; their positions, the signs they occupy, and the aspects formed from one to another all play a part in the make-up. The calculation and interpretation of these movements, the work of the astrologer, will produce an individual's birth chart. Because the heavens are constantly changing, people with identical birth charts are a very rare occurrence, although it could happen with people born at the same time and in the same place. In such a case the deciding factors as to how those individuals differ in their lives, loves, careers, financial prospects and so on would be due to environmental and parental influences.

Returning to the hypothetical Taurean: as has been said he would believe himself typical of the sign; but were the Moon and the Ascendant in the alternative positions stated he would be an Aquarian. So he would get a more dependable reading from the general Aquarian predictions than from the Taurean ones. This explains why some people swear by their newspaper horoscopes, their 'stars', while others can never believe them. But whatever his Moon sign and Ascendant, the Taurean will always display certain characteristics of his birth sign, because of the Sun's influence.

Belief in astrology does not necessarily mean believing we lead totally determined lives, that we are 'fated', or that we have no control over our destiny. What it shows is that our lives run in cycles, for good and for bad; knowing this, with the help of astrology we can make the most of, or minimize, certain patterns and tendencies. How this is done is entirely up to the individual.

For instance, if you know beforehand that you have a lucky period ahead, you can make the most of it by pushing ahead with plans and aspirations – anything that is dear to you. It follows that you can also restrain times of illness, misfortune, romantic upsets and everyday adversities.

Astrology should be used as it was originally intended – as a guide, especially to character. Throughout the ages there has never been found a better guide to character analysis, enabling people to learn and use advantageously the information relating to personality, friendships, work and romance.

Once this invaluable information has been understood it makes it easier for us to see ourselves as we really are, and what's more, as others see us. We can accept our own weaknesses and limitations and those of others. We can evolve from there to inner peace and outer confidence.

In the following pages you will find character guides, both 'positive' and 'negative', a health guide, how children can be helped by the use of astrology, your prospects in partnership and romance. Used wisely, astrology can help you through life. It is not a substitute to encourage complacency, since in the final analysis it all comes down to you. Allow astrology to walk hand in hand with you and success and happiness are virtually guaranteed.

Teri King

General Analysis

Positive characteristics

This type's greatest gift is a breadth of vision coupled with an unbiased and open mind. The Aquarian is unmoved by authority and, when faced with it, regards it with a certain amount of serenity and friendly interest. This character has an eagerness to learn from the fellow man, and can look at life from the outside rather than from the middle. Trust will only be placed in another person once that person has been investigated and studied and the actions and reasons for behaviour classified. However, should anyone else try these methods on the Aquarian he or she is not likely to be pleased.

Aquarians have a great feeling of warmth for mankind; they are humane in outlook and a friend to all. Their affections are well worth having, for they are the most sincere of people. However, they can be lonely on occasions for they find difficulty in settling down to steady relationships; loyalty is not a common thing.

The truth is all-important to them and a great amount of time is given up to the finding and telling of it. The roots of any relationship spring from friendship, for Aquarians tend to choose friends for their lovers.

Children love the Aquarian male, for they soon begin to realize that just about anything can happen around this character. Odd people come and go and he will have many strange interests.

The female of the species is attractive to the opposite sex. She has a delightful way of pointing out their assets, but not such charm when she also points out their weaknesses! A jealous man would be in for a shock if he should try to restrict her interests or contacts; she will dismiss him as quickly as dropping a hot cake. She rarely rushes into marriage and she can keep the hapless male waiting for years before the knot is finally tied. She has a cool façade that can be daunting to many males so that they will simply pass her by. She should look for a man with similar interests to her own in order to find complete happiness.

Negative characteristics

The wonderfully broad mind of this character can be wasted by covering too wide an area leading to inefficiency and loss of direction. Practical considerations of life will be lost in a mental haziness that clouds the many things he or she is capable of doing. The Aquarian will know what to do, but will be unable to find a place to begin. Wavering and time wasted over trifles often leads to lost opportunities. Aquarians have a certain lack of tact or consideration for others that leads to them blundering into difficulty. Their powers of concentration are almost non-existent. Unfortunately also, these weaker specimens can often be accused of cowardice.

Partnerships

Aquarius Woman

With Aries Man   (21 March to 20 April)
This woman, constantly surrounded by others in active debate, will attract Aries who likes activity of any description. Later he will find that her interest in others does not extend to him, and he is basically a self-centred person. This 'me first' attitude will be the basis for many arguments and, if she attacks his sensitive ego, all the force of his fiery temper will be directed at her. The Aquarian likes all relationships to be based on friendship but this is impossible for the Aries to accept, for he finds it impossible to make friends with those other than his own sex. Being a born leader he will resent the fact that she has every intention of following a career of her own. This will be further aggravated by the Arietian possessive streak, which makes him very reluctant to allow her to be involved in any task that does not involve him directly.

With Taurus Man   (21 April to 21 May)
Taurus is a character who enjoys his home life, a secure job and the respect of friends and acquaintances. To Aquarius these things are not important; she believes that her energies should be devoted to the good of mankind, not just the well being of one person. She will, for the most part, always be out and about getting involved in all kinds of causes and demonstrations. Here Taurus's jealousy will rear its ugly head, for he knows that whilst she is out, she is quite likely to meet a man who shares this interest. No doubt she will tell him at some point that his attitudes are wrong and that his priorities are somewhat mixed up. Not a well aspected partnership.

With Gemini Man   (22 May to 21 June)
There is a love of communication to this relationship and it will not be long before the two are totally involved in each other. If they do become absorbed in each other's interests a lot of fun will be had. Gemini is the original Jack of all Trades and this

will make finding a job rather difficult. The Aquarian also has weaknesses in this direction and this could, of course, lead to financial problems. A switching of roles could take place, each alternatively becoming the bread winner. She will have to decide, in the end, how the finances are to be handled and, providing she accepts this role, then the relationship could be very happy and stimulating for both parties.

With Cancer Man   (22 June to 22 July)
The Cancerian will appreciate this woman's air of efficiency and involvement, but it will not be until later that he discovers these attributes do not spill over into the domestic routine. He sets great store on his home environment, but she doesn't. Whisking through the housework at breakneck speed, doing only the barest necessities, will not meet with his approval. He feels that she should spend more time in the home rather than out with friends, doing them favours and joining in their meetings. He will even suggest that if she wants to change the world then she should start at home. She will not be amused by his suggestion. This is an unwise partnership, and one in which he is likely to get hurt, quite deeply.

With Leo Man   (23 July to 23 August)
This man has a knack of making people feel important, and this is the characteristic that will make him attractive to Miss Aquarius. Also, her absorption in life will equally attract him. However, his fiery pride and his love of the material things in life will give her much cause for complaint. Leo, being a passionate animal, will derive a lot of hurt and anguish from this detached woman, and his pride will make it almost impossible for him to get to the roots of her apparent coolness. If she fails to respond to his warmth and affection, he will turn to using arrogance and overbearance. She will have to cultivate an interest in the financial side of life, for Leo likes the best things in life even when he cannot afford them, so it would be wise for her to operate the purse strings. A very stormy partnership.

With Virgo Man   (24 August to 23 September)
Their love of communication could be the thing that brings these two together in the first place; she loves a man with a quick intelligent mind such as Virgo's. She is a reformer – trying to change the world into what she believes it should be. However,

whilst she is doing this, he will be trying to reform her. When she realizes this she will not be too happy about it. The biggest area of friction will be his critical eye, turned on her at every available opportunity. His insistence that she take on the role of housekeeper will unsettle and irritate her, for she will insist that household chores be shared, and besides this she has her own career to worry about. Her refusal to come to terms with his budgeting will also be an area for argument. A good friendship, but these two should never become lovers.

With Libra Man   (24 September to 23 October)
Libra's charm and apparent search for harmony will go to make an attractive package for the Aquarian. Her independence and her need for other people will lead him to try and make her a part of his life. She will want to remain independent and take part in the world around her. This won't bother him as long as she can remain feminine and well dressed. He will expect the relationship to remain on a romantic level and will do much to keep it this way. She will be happy with this arrangement as long as she can mildly flirt on occasions. Both are resilient types and should mix well with each other's friends. However, he could instigate worries over finances. On the whole, though, this is a good relationship.

With Scorpio Man   (24 October to 22 November)
The Aquarian woman, whilst famous for her adaptability, will find this relationship extremely hard going. His fixed opinions and intense emotions will not find favour with this humanitarian, especially where outside relationships are concerned. Jealousy is a major part of the Scorpio make-up; he believes it to be a necessary part of love. She, on the other hand, believes that it only serves to kill emotion. Therefore, her social life will cause him to feel resentment. She will never realize that self expression is impossible for him, and that his over-bearing attitude is only a need for reassurance. There also will be friction where finances are concerned, and her indifference to care with money will lead to many a scene. Also, her career will come in for some criticism, for he believes that she should be there at all times for his own exclusive use. These two will only serve to destroy each other.

With Sagittarius Man (23 November to 21 December)

Sagittarius will sense that love, in this woman's life, does not necessarily mean possession, therefore he will be attracted to her. She could easily be attracted to his love of challenge and adventure. This is a relationship in which each will be able to retain their individuality, and will be able to go their own way most of the time. The Sagittarian's emotions, which in general are short-lived, go very deep but her detached manner will sometimes stimulate him to find a warmer hearted person. There could also be chaos on the financial front. This will stem from the Sagittarian's tendency to gamble away the funds, and the Aquarian's lack of concern for the material things in life. The good news is that he will encourage and boost her career whenever possible, for he does not believe that the man should be the only one in a relationship with a career. A fair relationship, but one which swings from extreme to extreme.

With Capricorn Man (22 December to 20 January)

It is quite likely that a drifting Miss Aquarius will find herself rescued by this character. His responsible attitude to life will attract her and she will arouse his protective instincts. However, she will soon have to accept the fact that his career comes first, and the more interest she can show in it the better it will be for her. Whenever he sinks into a depression she will have to be there with encouragement. It is no use her being impatient with this pessimism, for that would only lead to violent quarrels. If harmony is to be achieved she will have to put her career second to his. He will object strongly when he finds that she has friends around at all hours, for he is not the sociable type. His tendency to save for the future will be encouraged by this woman who has no need for material things, but she could accuse him of being miserly. This is not a very satisfactory relationship.

With Aquarius Man (21 January to 19 February)

Intellectual compatibility may be the reason for the initial attraction in this case. Because other people believe that their cool façades mean they lack warmth, they will get satisfaction from each other by being able to drop this image together. The nurturing of this relationship should keep them both satisfied, as they both like to see human relationships develop. Life will be challenging for they will be constantly trying to keep up with each other, as she can change her moods and her mind as quickly as he. The financial aspect of the relationship could undermine compatibility, as neither will want to give this subject a lot of thought. However, someone will have to take charge of the purse strings. She will be able to follow her career, for he does not suffer feelings of inferiority, and he will support her in any way he can. This is a good union.

With Pisces Man   (20 February to 20 March)
The Piscean's feelings often show when he becomes involved with the affairs of other people, but not so the Aquarian's; she can help out in a detached manner devoid of all emotion. However, the Piscean will not realize this until he has known her for some time. He will believe that here is a true caring soul. In certain moods this man will adore being mothered by her, as she will sometimes adore mothering him. However, it may not always be so easy to get these moods to coincide. If he is desperate for warmth and she is not in the mood to give it, he could accuse her of being cold and heartless. This independent woman will be unable to comply with the wishes of the Piscean who likes to be the centre of his woman's world. She needs to develop her individuality and cannot fulfil this need if she has to think only of him. Money is an aspect of life both characters would prefer to ignore. However, the Aquarian usually possesses more common sense and it will fall to her to take care of the purse strings. This will be a difficult relationship.

Aquarius Man

With Aries Woman   (21 March to 20 April)
Miss Aries could find herself on the receiving end of this type's need to change everything. The Aquarian is a reformer; the type who will feel a need to change practically all he comes into contact with, be it his home, his office, his friends – the entire world. However, whilst all this change is going on it is rare that the Aquarian ever really improves anything. He knows what needs to be done, but cannot always find the necessary help to carry things through. Miss Aries will have to be a friend to this man as well as a lover. She also prefers the more sophisticated individuals peopling her world and will find it hard to come to terms with the eccentric types introduced to her by the Aquarian. The Aquarian is also known for his detached attitude to

Neptune – Your Ideals and Charm

Do you prefer the quiet life? Do you give the impression of being unworldly or absent-minded? Do others respond to your charms? Do you live up to the highest ideals? The influence of Neptune can affect all such behaviour.

If you have experienced strange and incomprehensible influences in your private or public life, then you need to understand whether Neptune is for or against you on your personal horoscope; with a little honesty, this should be easy to discover. Those with a strong Neptune are never ordinary types, but tend to be unique personalities with characteristics which are different and distinct from other beings. They are outstanding and often somewhat strange.

If Neptune works well for you then you understand life's meaning in an ideal or spiritual sense. If against, then you tend not to enjoy normal sensual pleasures, in which case you have a longing for the distortion of alcohol or drugs – anything to erase the boundaries between the fantastic and the real.

But whether for or against you, you will have a desire for higher perfection, unattainable in everyday life. Those with a strong Neptune prefer to do things backwards or upside-down – or in any way other than the usual. They love to pretend, to be something they are not, to reverse relationships between what they are and what they now tend to be. On a bad chart Neptune is a prime example of trickery and deceit.

One of this planet's most outstanding gifts is its formidable charm. Sometimes this is superficial and only a façade to cloak the insincere. In other cases, it is the outward and visible expression of true inner grace and shows itself in the kindest consideration for other people's feelings, being almost supernatural in its depth of understanding.

In a musical sense, a strong Neptune makes its owner highly-strung and sensitive. Such a person cannot stand long arduous strains as can others, and too much pressure over an extended period results in nervous problems.

A good Neptune will make you gentle and unassuming; you like to preserve the illusion of graciousness and charm. You are likely to need solitude and silence to nurture the inner being. Your sense of rythmn will be well developed. When working against you, Neptune can make you nervous and easily upset. If your environment is not congenial, you tend not to make any changes, but instead to retreat into a dream world where everything is well and happy. You may also tend towards hypochondria and are prone to complaints in which imagination and worry cause serious physical complications. But it does take approximately fourteen years for Neptune to pass through any sign; therefore, it is true that the sign your Neptune is in applies to your entire generation.

Now let us consider some of the positions of Neptune through the signs during this particular century.

Neptune in Cancer

Neptune in this particular sign encourages you to be receptive and psychic rather than dynamic or positive. Remember that Cancer is a Moon sign and its negative side can make those with Neptune under its influence more placid and variable than in other signs. There's a love of luxury and comfort, but a tendency to dissipate rather than build.

Neptune, like the sea, charms while it wears away cliffs by its continuous action. Cancer is also the sign of motherhood, so you are expected to be the kind of parent who is placid, charming and easy, but there will be a tendency to be over-indulgent. Unless there are stronger influences on your chart, you are unlikely to discipline children sufficiently or to strengthen their characters by good early training.

However, if Neptune is well aspected in Cancer, home-making will be a sacred art and you will provide your family with every comfort and endow your home with a special charm. In the home itself, every electrical appliance which contributes to the housewife's ease will have been considered a necessity and many in your generation will have profited by supplying a variety of household aids to a public which is eager to use them. At the same time, your generation would have taken an interest in antiques; with Neptune well aspected you would have embellished your home with furniture and objets d'art from other areas, or else reproductions of such items.

Such people possess a knack of taking the public's pulse and know both how to create and how to satisfy popular demand. Politics is thus largely coloured by sentimentality and you will possess a certain obstinacy in outlook. Great loyalty to party and past tradition or an appeal to the emotions on whichever side you may be, is typical – as is a certain personal conceit, especially when Neptune is afflicted.

Neptune was in Cancer from July 19 1901 to December 25 1901, May 21 1902 to September 23 1914, December 15 1914 to July 19 1915.

Neptune in Leo

This placing of Neptune points to noble ideals coupled with the ability to turn your dreams into reality. Neptune here tends to produce leaders who can arouse the masses – that is, heroes who have an emotional appeal. Those with Neptune thus placed are likely to inspire hero worship. Leo is the sign of children's schools and consequently the confusing and often hazy Neptune in this placing would sometimes have an adverse affect on education. Some born with Neptune in this position were the first to receive the so-called progressive education, often with detrimental results.

Neptune is the sign of drama, so amongst those who possess Neptune in Leo there are outstanding playwrights and actors as well as other literary figures who write to entertain.

Neptune was in Leo in the twenties when stock market speculation reached fever pitch and became a popular form of gambling rather than serious investment.

Those with Neptune in Leo will be fascinated by the romance and excitement of speculation, and although other aspects on their charts will make them turn their interest to the more solid and less glamorous aspects of speculation, they will still be charmed with the idea of a fantastic growth overnight.

When Neptune works well, many of you will realize your ambitions in this respect. But a badly placed Neptune gives a lazy personality, a love of luxury and an indication to be weak and cowardly or else self-centred and something of a bully. When well placed, it produces imperious, daring, fiery, masterful and often radical people who will go to great lengths to further their ideals.

Neptune was in Leo from September 24 1914 to December 14 1914, from July 19 1915 to March 18 1916, from May 2 1916 to September 20 1928, from February 19 1929 to July 23 1929.

Neptune in Virgo

Virgo is material and Neptune is a spiritual planet, hence a combination of the two gives an almost psychic understanding of situations and people. When Neptune is well placed, you do not have to see something with your own eyes in order to understand what is going on; you are able to see it in your mind's eye. A well-aspected Neptune in Virgo gives practical ability to command organizational projects. These people are at their best able to conceive the plans for tremendous building complexes and shopping centres. They are constructive either in the sense of being architects and planners or by way of active participation in the building process. On the other hand, they may live in such projects, which for them would have a special charm.

But when Neptune works against you, you have odd concepts connected with work, and may feel you should be taken care of even if you deliberately choose not to earn your own living. This of course does not refer to those who are disabled or unable to contribute to their own support for valid reasons. An afflicted Neptune means that even when you do work, you can be lazy and simply pass your time physically in the place of employment without taking an active interest or trying to do a good job. At heart, such people feel the world owes them a living and they are out to collect it with the least possible inconvenience.

However, a well-placed Neptune in Virgo produces the opposite behaviour. These people romanticize their work and are tremendously capable. They are as conscientious and as careful of details as those with a badly-placed Neptune are careless.

Those of the generation born with Neptune in Virgo tend to romanticize scientific research and to scoff at spiritual values for which there is no apparent physical proof. This is, nevertheless, a good influence for scientists, since it gives them keen analytical powers and an understanding of material things. It is also a good position for writers, making them perceptive and able to express themselves with a special charm. Their report on reality is precise and true to life. It is also a powerful constructive influence for musicians and artists.

Neptune was in Virgo from September 21 1928 to Feruary 19 1929. July 24 1929 to October 3 1942, April 17 1943 to August 2 1943.

Neptune in Libra

Those of you with Neptune in Libra will be only too aware that this planet is one of aspiration and high ideals. Put into practice your concepts of peace and equality and you could change the world. However, this does not give you much force and you tend to use forms of passive resistance – such as sit-ins, marches and other demonstrations – to further your objectives. Not surprisingly to astrologers, you have been called 'the love generation'. Libra is the sign of Venus the planet of Love, and the idea of universal love is most natural to those of you with Neptune so placed. However, Neptune is also the planet of hazy ideas and illusions, and many of you may discover that your ideal of love can vanish like a mirage. You must learn that love often demands sacrifice and that to sustain love one must have a mature acceptance of responsibility.

Libra is the sign of marriage, and those with Neptune so placed can expect to revolutionize this institution. Marriage as we know it today will be a thing of the past to your age group. Old customs will come under scrutiny and be discarded for a change.

Many of the nineteenth-century poets were born under this influence. And like them, many of you will express yourselves in writing and speech with unusual charm, beauty and grace. However, when Neptune is badly placed, you may expect many exaggerations and strange abuses in literature and art. You will be concerned with the refinement of manners. The outer forms of expressed behaviour will fascinate you and while you will reject the standards of the past in many instances, you will take from compatible sources and transform them into rituals of your own.

Those with Neptune in Libra are truly children of the space age. Your scientific discoveries will be phenomenal, and you will participate in explorations which will colonize other planets. You will take to space with the same spirit that Columbus took to the sea.

Neptune was in Libra from October 4 1942 to April 16 1943, from August 3 1943 to December 23 1955, March 12 1956 to October 18 1956, June 16 1957 to August 5 1957.

Neptune in Scorpio

Those with Neptune in Scorpio are likely to possess a very vivid imagination. Because of this you will be responsive to the psychic, the occult and to any form of subtle stimuli. You have the ability to investigate and transpose. Emotionally speaking, you are intense and extremely passionate. Neptune in Scorpio will probably make you very sensual, but you are likely to be intemperate and on occasions downright perverse. This placing will inhibit your partiality. You must make concerted efforts not to be too opinionated. In many instances, the imagination is so strong that you will be prone to having vivid dreams and practical occult experiences. This is a good placing for marriage, money, partnership and legacies; unless badly aspected, in which case the opposite will apply. Neptune in this placing is at best subtle and at worse cruel. And those with Neptune in Scorpio are likely to be fascinated by revolutions, stimulated by exposing something previously hidden from the public. Allied to a sense of social justice – and it is likely to be – this can be harnessed to achieve much to the public good. With a bad aspect, children with Neptune in Scorpio will need very careful direction, especially if cruel or underhand tendencies begin to emerge.

Neptune was in Scorpio December 24 1955 to March 11 1956, from October 19 1956 to June 1957, from August 5 1957 to January 5 1970 and from May 3 1970 to November 6 1970.

Punters' Luck for 1986

Flat Jockeys for 1986 Season – Lucky Dates

WILLIE CARSON 27th March; 1st – 3rd, 9th, 10th, 19th, 20th April; 14th, 23rd, 24th May; 11th, 18th, 21st June; 1st, 14th, 26th July; 1st, 10th, 14th August; 10th, 16th, 23rd, 26th September; 13th, 26th, 31st October; 1st November.

JOHN REID 19th, 20th March; 1st, 4th April; 12th, 30th May; 4th, 10th, 26th June; 19th, 25th July; 6th, 21st, 28th, 29th August; 24th, 25th September; 10th, 17th–25th October, 4th November.

B. JOHNSON 4th, 18th April; 12th, 13th, 15th, 16th May; 10th, 25th, 28th (very good) June; 1st–12th July inclusive; 12th, 19th, 24th, 26th, 27th, 31st August; 10th, 11th, 15th September; 4th, 12th, 13th October; 10th, 12th November.

BRYAN ROUSE 21st, 28th, 29th March; 17th, 18th April; 10th, 17th, 21st May; 16th, 27th June; 2nd, 22nd, 23rd, 29th July; 8th, 12th (very good) August; 5th, 7th, 9th, 23rd September; 20th–23rd, 24th October.

N. CARLYLE 18th, 26th, 28th March; 7th, 24th April; 10th, 16th, 19th, 26th, 27th May; 2nd, 10th, 15th, 27th June; 6th, 11th, 16th, 29th July; 16th, 17th, 29th, 31st (very good) August; 1st, 2nd, 14th, 29th September, 8th, 17th, 19th, 29th October.

RICHARD FOX 15th (very good), 18th March; 6th, 12th, 22nd, 25th, 30th April; 15th, 16th, 19th, 24th May; 8th, 10th, 15th, 26th June; 6th, 16th July; 2nd, 11th, 28th August; 11th, 13th, 17th, 27th September; 10th, 17th, 23rd, 28th October.

RICHARD HILLS 21st March; 11th, 19th, 22nd, 30th April; 8th, 12th, 16th, 23rd May; 12th, 17th, 28th, 29th June; 4th and 5th (very good), 13th, 25th July; 10th, 14th, 25th August; 15th, 25th, 27th September; 10th–14th inclusive, 20th October.

MICHAEL HILLS 25th March; 4th, 10th, 18th April; 1st, 11th,

13th, 17th, 31st May; 8th, 9th, 11th, 17th, 25th June; 3rd, 13th, 29th July; 13th, 24th, 25th, 27th August; 9th, 13th September; 12th–18th inclusive, 19th October; 1st–8th November inclusive.

STEVE CAUTHEN 4th, 5th, 8th, 23rd April; 9th, 27th May; 9th, 18th, 25th, 29th June; 1st, 5th–19th July (very good month); 1st–11th, 26th, 27th August; 11th, 16th September; 9th (very good), 17th–25th inclusive, 26th, 27th October; 1st–9th November.

P. ROBINSON 10th, 17th May; 28th, 29th, 30th June; 1st, 29th July; 31st August; 2nd, 9th, 12th, 13th, 17th, 18th September; 9th, 12th–18th October inclusive.

W. SWINBURN 18th, 25th March; 5th, 22nd, 23rd, 24th April; 9th, 16th, 25th (very good) May; 7th, 12th, 26th, 27th, 28th June; 1st–6th, 7th, 27th July (good month); 2nd, 11th, 27th August; 12th, 14th–20th inclusive, 27th, 29th September; 7th, 16th, 23rd, 24th October.

PAT EDDERY 26th March; 11th, 19th, 24th–26th April; 1st, 2nd, 6th, 13th, 16th, 17th May; 1st–7th inclusive, 11th, 12th, 30th June; 2nd, 12th, 17th, 29th July; 12th, 13th, 24th, 27th, 28th August; 12th, 13th, 18th, 19th, 27th September; 10th–18th October (particularly good, but the whole month is generally good); 1st–7th November.

M. STALTE 25th, 29th March; 11th, 19th, 24th April; 9th, 10th, 20th May; 9th, 10th, 25th, 26th, 27th–30th June; 15th, 17th, 27th July; 1st–5th, 11th (especially good), 14th (especially good), August; 6th (especially good), 17th (especially good), 22nd, 27th (especially good), September; 2nd, 15th October; 4th, 5th November.

DAVID O'BRIEN 24th, 31st March; 18th, 20th April; 20th, 24th May; 4th, 18th (very good), 19th, 30th June; 1st, 11th, 18th, 26th (very good) July; 14th, 15th, 20th, 29th August; 1st, 11th, 17th, 26th September; 6th, 14th, 15th, 21st, 28th October.

GUY HARWOOD 8th, 18th, 30th April; 10th, 11th, 15th, 16th, 19th–22nd, 30th May; 9th, 13th June; 7th, 11th, 18th, 22nd, 28th (especially good) July; 3rd, 25th August; 1st–4th, 8th, 11th (especially good), 13th (especially good), 15th September; 12th, 15th October.

PAUL KELLAWAY 5th, 8th, 20th, 24th, 28th April; 5th, 6th, 15th 17th, 20th May; 18th June; 2nd, 14th, 18th, 26th July; 7th, 19th, 27th, 31st August; 2nd, 9th, 10th, 15th, 16th, 17th September; 8th October.

JOHN SUTCLIFFE 22nd March (very good); 1st, 11th, 19th (very good), April; 13th, 23rd May; 2nd, 6th, 16th, 23rd June; 12th, 21st, 24th, 25th July; 9th, 13th, 24th, 25th August; 8th, 15th, 21st, 24th September; 4th, 10th, 25th, 27th October.

CLIVE BRITTAIN 24th March; 4th, 9th, 14th, 15th, 17th, 24th April; 1st, 9th, 12th, 17th, 30th May; 6th, 10th, 17th June; 3rd, 4th, 5th, 11th, 28th July (good month); 11th, 12th, 24th, 26th August; 12th, 16th, 17th, 18th, 26th (very good), 30th September; 12th October (in general, good early in month); 8th November.

GAVIN PRITCHETT GORDON 29th, 31st March; 1st, 11th, 12th, 15th, 22nd April; 3rd, 5th, 11th, 13th, 27th, 28th, 30th May; 1st, 10th, 25th (very good), 30th June; 19th, 31st July; 4th, 15th and 16th August (very good), 18th, 29th August (good mid-month); 17th, 18th, 20th, 21st September; 1st (very good), 4th, 12th, 23rd, 27th, 28th October; 1st November.

BARRY HILLS 18th March; 1st, 6th, 8th, 9th, 10th, 25th, 26th April; 3rd, 6th, 10th, 18th–24th May; 2nd, 4th, 8th, 12th, 19th, 27th June; 19th, 26th, 28th July; 15th, 19th August; 3rd, 9th, 13th, 17th September; 7th, 12th, 26th, 28th October; 1st November.

JOHNSON HOUGHTON 21st March (very good); 2nd, 17th, 19th, 20th, 30th April; 7th, 12th, 18th (very good), 21st, 22nd May; 12th, 13th, 16th (very good), 19th, 23rd, 27th June; 23rd (very good), 31st July; 8th, 11th (very good), 14th, 25th August; 7th, 10th, 14th, 15th, 23rd September; 4th, 10th, 15th, 24th October.

M. A. JARVIS 26th March; 1st, 7th, 13th, 16th, 25th April; 1st, 9th, 24th, 26th May; 8th, 9th–14th inclusive, 27th June; 1st, 4th, 15th, 28th July; 10th, 12th, 15th, 28th August; 18th, 28th September, 3rd, 22nd, 23rd October, 6th, 7th November.

R. ARMSTRONG 12th, 15th, 22nd, 23rd April; 15th, 16th, 17th, 19th, 29th May; 2nd, 11th, 12th, 16th, 22nd June; 7th, 17th, 18th, 31st July; 18th, 27th August; 1st, 2nd, 12th, 18th, 29th, 30th September; 1st, 2nd, 18th, 24th October.

Your Pets and Astrology

Aries 21 March to 20 April
On the credit side, your Aries pet will be affectionate, warm and extremely loyal. However, an inability to learn from past mistakes can lead to training problems and great patience is therefore required in this respect. Healthwise, such an animal is invariably accident-prone and physical safety is constantly endangered by its own tendency towards haste and impulse. The physical area most in jeopardy is the head. Keep a vigilant watch on this part of the body. With this advice borne in mind, your companion will lead a long, happy life.

Taurus 21 April to 21 May
No training problems here; the Taurean pet is naturally obedient. The only exception is on occasions when the Taurean stubborness is rampant. Take your pet for a walk, throw a stick for him to retrieve and for no obvious reason he will suddenly sit down as if rooted to the spot, looking you up and down as if to say, 'You fetch it, I'm simply not in the mood.' The same applies to the feline of the species. 'Have you any idea how stupid you look crawling around with that piece of string?' her expression seems to say. Coax and cajole all you like, but your Taurean pet won't budge when its mind is set against doing so. But at least there is no problem where food is concerned, for this animal loves to satiate itself. There is nothing so content as a well-fed Taurean. However, do guard against gluttony, for this could obviously undermine health.

Gemini 22 May to 21 June
The Geminian pet is pure joy – ever-ready for a game and with a delightfully wicked sense of humour. This animal refuses to grow up, and at fifteen and even later will chase a ball just as energetically as it did when a small kitten or puppy. This type is very erratic and tends to eat when it wants to, with the result that it is often a nibbler. Sleep and exercise are also taken according to mood: one day lazy and constantly snoozing, to the point where you suspect something must be wrong, and the

next zooming around like a maniac with no thought for rest at all. Because of this, owners need to keep an eye on food intake and exercise, for although this animal will never admit to it, Geminians do need the correct diet and exercise in order to stay healthy.

Cancer 22 June to 22 July
The Cancerian animal makes an excellent family pet. It takes a maternal interest in every single member of the family and can fret to the point of extreme when someone is absent. Whether feline or canine this animal loves water, especially if introduced to it at an early age. Furthermore, it has a sweet tooth, but before you allow your pet to indulge in left-over desserts or to nibble at bars of chocolate, bear in mind that those precious teeth have to last a long time. Therefore, unless you can train your pet to brush its teeth, you would be extremely unwise to encourage this side of its character. Healthwise the stomach is often delicate but quick to recuperate from any problems.

Leo 23 July to 23 August
This animal instinctively knows how to put most humans in their places. Never lose sight of the fact that you are dealing with royalty and as such the Leo type demands the respect it innately knows to be its right. Therefore, discourage children from dressing up the family pet; it will never forgive you and may pack a bundle in a spotted handkerchief and leave home! When training, play on the Achilles' heel of Leo subjects – namely a love of flattery. Constantly tell your pet how beautiful, brave, or clever he or she is and watch the response. You will no doubt bore your friends by relating tales of how your animal seems to know every word you say and so it does – especially when it comes to extolling his/her virtues. Healthwise, this type has two extremes: either never ill or else always on the sick list. Pay special attention to the back, for this is the Leo's vulnerable area.

Virgo 24 August to 23 Sept
If you are a slob, then you would be very ill-advised to purchase a Virgoan pet, since your untidiness could cause a nervous breakdown. Drop a sock or stocking on the floor and you will experience a hot sensation at the back of the neck; turn round and you are faced with a pair of indignant, accusing eyes. Better

pick up the offending item at once! The Virgoan animal is fastidious both with food and physical cleanliness. Cranky food habits are expected and you will not change this, so accept it. Ideally this type makes a great pet for those living alone. It is intelligent, playful but somewhat nervous; therefore noisy children are difficult for it to accept. Healthwise, keep an alert eye open for skin and bowel problems.

Libra   24 Sept to 23 Oct
If you want an animal who will fit in with almost any situation, then this is your pet. Not because it is so adaptable, but more due to the fact that it is often too lazy to protest at any change. This therefore makes it an ideal family pet, but do ensure that children do not take advantage of its easygoing nature. Invariably this is an affectionate, sensible and devoted pet. Food presents little or no complications as this type devours anything; not surprisingly, in many cases this tendency can lead to a weight problem in later life. The Libran weak spot is the kidneys, so owners are advised to keep a wary eye open for any troubles in this direction and always ensure that your pet has easy access to fresh water. This will help to minimize health problems.

Scorpio   24 Oct to 22 Nov
If your pet loves you and is born under the sign of Scorpio, then you have complete devotion; but if for some reason you don't come up to scratch, then he or she will be off. Therefore you need to shape up before it's too late. Jealousy can also present you with a hazard. A new baby – or worse still, a new pet – will cause this kind to pine and liberal amounts of love will be needed if it is to accept the intruder. Maybe it never will do so, but at least an uneasy truce can be achieved if you know how to handle this particular type. Being a water subject, your pet will drink gallons of it and love to be in or near it. Therefore, no problems are expected when it comes to bathtime, quite the reverse. Such enthusiasm can lead to one hell of a mess and cover everything within a six-foot radius. Healthwise, the Scorpio rules the genitals and infections there are fairly common. Much depends on whether the animal is spayed or left intact. Not a pet for the faint-hearted.

Sagittarius   23 Nov to 21 Dec
This is the real sport of the zodiac, and the more fresh air and exercise the better – therefore not an ideal pet to own if you live in a poky flat or bedsitter. Such an animal would be most distressed in such circumstances. Besides, this has got to be the clumsiest animal ever, so that a small living area could spell nothing short of disaster. Furthermore, even those living in spacious houses should put delicate furniture well out of reach; this animal can't help it, no matter how much training it receives. The Sagittarian pet is an adaptable sort. It will accept new members of the family with glee and a move of house is regarded as a wild adventure – no pining for the old home here. A great family pet then, full of life and fun.

Capricorn   22 Dec to 20 January
This is the sign of the late developer, therefore owners must not fret if such an animal is slow to mature either physically or mentally. This type is a fighter, one who will put up with almost anything and remain loyal. It does possess one fault, however, and that is a tendency to snobbishness. No one is better than HIS FAMILY and visitors are viewed with disdain; this is especially applicable if your pet be feline. Foodwise there are no problems and in this particular area, discrimination flies out of the window. Furthermore the pet under this sign will be somewhat reserved; certainly it loves you but has no need to make a fool of itself when showing this. Healthwise, owners need to be watchful for dental problems, colds and accidents to the knees. But in the main, this is usually a healthy and long-lived specimen.

Aquarius   21 January to 19 February
This too can be the detached type. There will be times when a vacant look enters your pet's eyes and you may come to the conclusion that he or she is just plain stupid. Little do you realize that this animal has probably just worked out a chemical cure for some disease, or invented the first robot replica of itself for companionship's sake. Furthermore, this is the sign of the logical thinker, so don't try to con such an animal and never be condescending. This type has a great sense of fun, so Aquarian animals make excellent family pets. Healthwise, problems associated with the eyes or circulation should never be neglected, for these are the Aquarian's vulnerable areas.

Pisces 20 February to 20 March

This type can only be an ideal family pet where there are older children. Little tots can be so cruel and here it must be borne in mind that we are dealing with a most sensitive sign. Your pet will always be ready to be treated like a baby, with lots of attention and love. Obviously, then, a home which is frequently empty such as a bachelor pad would be most unsuitable; the animal might stray and would fret exceedingly. Physically the Pisces pet appears delicate and even fragile, when in actual fact the constitution can often match that of an ox. Be sure that food and drink are always fresh, since this could represent a health hazard. Bullying of any description is ill-advised and may actually cause illness. Training should be undertaken with a firm but gentle hand for the best results. Never lose sight of the fact that this animal wants to please; it is his/her mission in life, so don't be too hard on the Pisces pet.

Compatibilities

Two animals are frequently twice as much fun as one. But when choosing a companion for your pet, life can be made considerably easier if you select one of its astrological compatibles. See the list below.

Fire signs: Aries, Leo and Sagittarius (all compatible).
Water signs: Cancer, Scorpio, Pisces (all compatible).
Air signs: Gemini, Libra, Aquarius (all compatible).
Earth signs: Taurus, Virgo, Capricorn (all compatible).

Spaying or doctoring should not be undertaken when the moon is in the following signs: Scorpio, Libra, Virgo. During these periods, complications are likely to occur. Refer to the tables at the back of the book.

The Year in Focus

Last year was pretty good to you, wasn't it? This was thanks to Jupiter. This year, however, you can only continue to rely on good fortune until February 21st, when Jupiter will move out of your sign into Pisces. Although the opportunities for expansion that have existed will no longer apply, at least Pisces is the financial area of your chart and therefore you should be providentially protected from any serious harm with the possible exception of waste – but that's up to you.

The placing of Saturn continuing in Sagittarius indicates that you somehow manage to gather responsibility in connection with friends. It is also a pointer to the fact that all your more experienced and older friends can offer you some good advice, so do not hesitate to go to them.

Pluto continues to wreak havoc through the zenith of your chart, making it difficult for you to feel secure at your place of work. However, try to bear in mind that this is also the position of power and it is quite likely that many of you will rise considerably in status and prestige during the year ahead.

Romantically it is not really a year for settling down. Uranus continues to bring sudden attractions and equally sudden repulsions into your life, therefore, it is most likely you will be playing the field. However, there will be exceptions to this which are covered in the ensuing pages.

Therefore, 1986 looks as if it will be a good year for you, but of course it is up to you to make the most of it. Now read on.

January

For you the year begins slowly. An anti-social and depressive mood slowly shifts, but does not completely disappear until the 19th has passed. Once this date arrives, the Sun and Venus enter your sign and you will be full of confidence, sociability, charm and romance. Those of you who are professionally involved in work that could be described as behind the scenes, or in anything on the creative side, can expect a spectacular month. But for all the workload promises to be extremely heavy, thanks to Mars' placing at the zenith of your chart. Make sure you set aside some periods for real relaxation, otherwise you just won't be able to cope. The full Moon on the 26th is an indication that a relationship is about to come to an end. A little later you will be glad it happened. This month therefore is cleanly cut in two, the third and fourth weeks being infinitely more interesting and eventful than the first fortnight.

February

This must be one of the most important months of the year, with the second and third weeks emphasized, thanks to the fact that the Sun will be in conjunction with Jupiter. It is likely that many of you will have decided on a late winter wedding. For others, that special someone finally comes along, or you may be one of the Aquarians for whom there is some surprisingly good news in connection with either your career or money. Whichever way, this is not bad, is it? If you are professionally involved with the law and allied occupations, now is a particularly good time. Socially speaking, Mars enters Sagittarius indicating that you are eager to make new friends; the male sex will be particularly helpful and important to you regardless of whether you yourself are male or female. Financially, you seem to gain through a document or contract, and there are some unexpected presents as well as long-overdue cheques which finally arrive. The new Moon in your sign on the 9th hails the beginning of a minor new cycle in life, and the full Moon on the 24th indicates the end of a problem connected with officialdom. Do make the most of this month – in many ways it could not be better.

March

Under normal circumstances one could hardly describe you as a materialistic type. However, with three planets sailing through the money area of your chart, that is how you are going to be for approximately four weeks, and because of this you make some startling progress where funds are concerned. The new Moon on the tenth of the month is an indication of a fresh source of income. Therefore, if you are unemployed, for heaven's sake get out and about on this day. Take care romantically, however, for it is quite likely that a new member of the opposite sex will have ulterior motives behind their attachment to you. Yours is the sign of the truth seeker, so turn the spotlight of truth on him or her. If you are a sporty type, you will be attending a social function in connection with a club – or maybe even organising it very satisfactorily. Affairs connected with relatives, especially a brother or sister, are also well-starred; also, some recent problem in connection with them is cleared out of the way. The housewife is likely to be in the mood for bargain-hunting and should be lucky in this particular direction. Socially you will be prepared to be more adventurous and go further afield for entertainment, and you will thoroughly enjoy yourself. It is not a time for home entertaining, so get out as much as possible. A good month.

April

With the Sun and Mercury sailing through Aries, this is an excellent month for all those involved in transport, communications, publishing, the literary world or travel. A good time also for the bargain-hunter. Get out and prowl around those secondhand shops – you might find something special. For all, it is a time of rushing around, to-ing and fro-ing. You will be prepared to go further afield for your personal, private, and professional lives and will thoroughly enjoy the experience. In fact you will be downright bored at home. Your monetary planet Neptune is in backward action at the moment, therefore finances could get a little involved – try not to take on any further commitments, especially hire purchase arrangements. Venus' placing in the second house indicates that the need to beautify your surroundings becomes stronger as the month passes, and money will be spent on this. For the younger reader who is needing a time to approach parents, this is an excellent time for doing just that. You can bridge the generation gap in one fell swoop. Romantically you are unlikely to come across anything greatly significant, although there are many casual encounters indicated. Careerwise, my best advice to you is not to make waves, but to keep yourself in the background and do your job properly. There seems to be a change in your place of work and you need to make sure that this does not relate to you. The full Moon on the 24th, in Scorpio, is an indication that you are coming to the end of a minor cycle, where your career is concerned. This may involve a move from one department to another, or indeed to a new job. An excellent time also for seeking employment.

May

May is a month which is particularly kind to all of you who are involved in property affairs and the allied professions. It is also an excellent time for those moving house or house-hunting. Although you may step outside occasionally in order to socialize, in the main you will be quite happy to stay at home and indulge in your pet hobbies – whoever he or she might be! The new Moon in Taurus on the 8th is an indication of changes within the home environment and a minor new cycle. The full Moon on the 23rd backs up the fact that there are changes going on in your place of work, but there is no need for you to panic – you will be more adaptable than you believed possible. Healthwise you are in A1 condition. Romantically there are few chances, I'm afraid, therefore this is a month which tends to favour the married Aquarian.

June

Almost exclusively, this is a month for enjoyment. It is also a good time for those of you professionally involved in entertainment, speculation, children, animals and sport. If the former applies to you, you can expect extra money or promotion. Parents find children easier to cope with and may actually enjoy their company. Furthermore you will be surprised when you discover that running around with the children for the sake of their social life is not quite such a bore as you thought it would be. For the single though, it is mainly a time for having fun and kicking up your heels. Do not take yourself too seriously on an emotional level, for you will be in and out of love almost before you have had time to effect an introduction. Workwise, the atmosphere and environment at work seem to be changing for the better as does your relationship with your workmates. Healthwise, there seems to be trouble with your nerves as well as through over-indulgence. This is hardly surprising – try to keep a sense of moderation. Financially, Neptune continues its backward action, therefore refrain from taking on more financial commitments. Jupiter is there to protect you unless you insist on being downright stupid. The new Moon on the 7th in Gemini points to the end of a minor cycle in connection with a love affair, and the full Moon on the 22nd promises to bring a change of heart or mind.

July

After all the recent fun and games of last month, you might be quite happy to settle down to some work – a fact your boss might be glad to hear about. However, concentration is not going to be that easy, for Mercury opposes you throughout the month and you will find your mind shifting away from whatever it is you have in hand. Much depends on how much self-discipline you have. If you are married, partners will be in a restless mood and it will take all of your time and energy to keep up with them. This promises to be a rather exhausting month, therefore you would be well advised not to plan too hectic a social life – you will need time to restore your energy and recuperate from the activity that is going on outside the home. One of the brighter points of the month is that Venus' placing makes it an excellent time for handling official-dom, legal affairs or the bank manager. If you have problems in these areas then do act after the 12th. The new Moon in Cancer on the 7th points to changes at work, perhaps a new member of the staff; whoever he or she is, a business relationship is likely to turn into a romantic one.

August

Not the best time of the year for you. You are an independent soul, and with the Sun and Mercury in your opposition, it is hardly the time for branching out on your own – neither is it particularly lucky for the freelance worker. Those who benefit most will be Aquarians who are happy to work in harness, or who form a professional partnership. Mercury continues to oppose you from the 13th onwards, therefore nerves are still slightly tender and you would be well-advised to concentrate your social life around those whose company you enjoy and whose personality you find compatible. The position of Mars in Capricorn is an indication that you may find relatives somewhat trying during the month ahead, and you will need all your tact and diplomacy – or rather, your partner's tact and diplomacy – if you are to avoid serious disagreement. On a romantic level, unless you are involved with a foreigner or you have the good fortune to find one, I am afraid it is a rather quiet time and the married Aquarians clearly fare the best. For the single, the new Moon on the 5th in Leo is a clear indication that a romance is in the offing. The full Moon on the 22nd in Aries points to the fact that you should find a ready solution to a long-outstanding problem. Not a particularly exciting month.

September

With Mercury in the solar ninth house, it is quite likely that many of you will have decided to take a holiday late this year. If so, you have chosen well – it should be without complication, thoroughly enjoyable and provide you with many opportunities of meeting new people. Some of the relationships formed abroad are likely to last for some time. On a professional level, the month tends to favour those involved in big business, such as the Stock Exchange, building society, insurance etc. For others, it is an excellent time for dealing with those involved in such professions. Also, Venus at the zenith of your chart is good news for all who are involved with the arts or creativity. It will be a good idea for you to combine business with pleasure at every opportunity; this will prove to be not only enjoyable but most rewarding. If you are unemployed, regardless of your sex you should listen to the females in your family circle – they will have some good ideas. And if you can, try to attend interviews around the 8th and 9th and the day of the full Moon on the 18th. Those of you expecting or hoping to hear from someone abroad, should be lucky during the month ahead; amongst the correspondence, there is likely to be a question which will need some careful consideration. Mars continuing in your solar twelfth house is still an indication that you need to tread carefully and warily where relatives are concerned.

October

After the 8th Mars enters your sign, and then you would be wise to bear in mind that this planet endows you with increased vitality, energy and enthusiasm. However, it is imperative that you find an outlet for all of this, otherwise these added characteristics will only deteriorate into tension, aggression and a need to quarrel with all and sundry. Furthermore, sexual passions will be on the increase; there is nothing wrong with this at all, so long as you do not mistake them for something more serious. Therefore, stay away from important or heavy commitments. On a professional level, the month favours those involved with the uniformed occupations, matters related to travel, foreigners, import, export etc. With Venus and Mercury continuing at the top of your chart, it is likely that changes are taking place at your work, but these should be to the good, so do not worry about them. The new Moon on the 2nd in Virgo is an indication that you will be receiving news from an official source. The full Moon in Cancer on the 24th points to the fact that health might not be too good on this day, although for the rest of the month you are in A1 condition.

November

This is an extremely ambitious time of year for you. Mars continues in your sign, meaning that you are ready to fight tooth and nail for everything you want on a professional level. And although considerable progress can be made in this particular direction, it is likely that personal relationships will suffer. If you are unemployed, now is the time to get to grips with interviews and letter-writing – the new Moon on the 2nd could very well bring you a fresh job. Those faring best will be Aquarians professionally connected with the arts, creativity, the luxury trades, the media, buying and selling. The full Moon on the 16th points to the end of a minor cycle in connection with family affairs. Socially life will only be active if you can manage to combine business with pleasure, for I fear you are interested in little else during the month ahead. Healthwise you are in A1 condition, which is more than can be said for the romantic side of your life.

December

After the coldness and ruthlessness of November, December will come as a pleasant change for those around you. The sociable side of your character surfaces once more, and you seem to be attending several functions in association with a club – probably a sporting club. New friends mean that you exchange ideas and from this stems a fresh objective in life. Mars has moved into your solar second house, making a hole in your pocket, but probably this is connected with Christmas. However, do be careful with possessions, for they will have a habit of disappearing or being caused to disappear. Romantically and socially, most of the activity and opportunities come to you in association with work or workmates. When the actual festive period arrives, you will feel the need to escape – let's hope you are spending Christmas away from home, otherwise you would become rather niggardly and difficult to please. The new Moon on the 1st brings a cycle of new friends and they will affect your life for some time to come. And the full Moon on the 16th means that you are reaching the end of a cycle in connection with children or, possibly, love affairs. By the time New Year's Eve arrives, in retrospect you will have decided the 1986 was not such a bad year after all, and will no doubt be eagerly awaiting 1987. MERRY CHRISTMAS!

Day-by-day Horoscope

January

1st – What started out yesterday as a minor disagreement could blow up into a major row today. Try not to lose your temper, as it would be pity to lose a close friend right now.

2nd – Expect the unexpected where a work colleague is concerned; it is quite likely that you will have the wind taken out of your sails by something he or she says.

3rd – Not a good day for thinking about your financial position. The thought of expenses over Christmas and the New Year will be depressing. Keep your mind on other things of a more pleasant nature.

4th – A good weekend for meeting up with friends and relatives, but do not become involved in expensive entertainment pursuits. There is as much fun to be had for nothing behind your own front door.

5th – Try to spend the day quietly, but if that is not possible meet up with friends of an intellectual bent rather than those who like to have a raucous and rowdy time.

6th – You will find it difficult to regain cash you lost some time ago, specially if you made a loan to a colleague. This afternoon is the best time to track down elusive superiors.

7th – Make the most of the opportunities that come your way. There could be something in the wind at your place of work which leads you to believe there is promotion on the way.

8th – Take careful notice of what others are doing at present – you could gain financially by becoming involved with their schemes. This evening is a good time for mixing business with pleasure.

9th – You may have thoughts of rearranging your household budget, but this will not meet with universal approval. You should consult with partners before tightening the purse-strings.

10th – Your workload will be heavier than normal and you will have difficulty in getting through the day. Enlist the help of colleagues if you are to complete all that you have been set.

11th – A good day for getting out and about, but you should wrap up against the elements as there is a danger of contracting colds and chills. Friends make ideal companions this evening.

12th – A good time for visiting relatives whom you have not seen for some time. But call up before you leave as otherwise you could find yourself knocking on the door of an empty house.

13th – Begin the week as you mean to carry on. The enterprising ones of this sign will be those who benefit today. Try to find ways of making some extra cash – younger people may have the answer.

14th – A feeling of depression will be lurking and you will be imagining the most dire things where friends and colleagues are concerned. Do not take your morbid fantasies too seriously.

15th – This is a day to push ahead with your plans and schemes for the future, if you feel up to it. A scheme that was launched some time ago could now be coming to fruition.

16th – Financial affairs will receive a boost owing to a cheque or other payment you have been waiting to drop through your letter-box. Try to be thrifty with your new-found wealth.

17th – This is an excellent day for dealing with the problems of family, especially if they concern off-spring. Make certain that you do not lecture them – rather, give advice in a friendly manner.

18th – Try to keep home life on an even keel, as there are likely to be one or two outbursts through the day. Relatives are argumentative and difficult to get along with. Remain calm at all times!

19th – A good day for getting together with work colleagues on a social level and discussing working conditions, plans and projects. You glean some useful information from someone older than yourself.

20th – Superiors are easily impressed today, so set about showing yourself off in the best possible light. Do not be too timid to blow your trumpet and wave your flag.

21st – Those attending job interviews and discussions can make their presence felt simply by speaking up at the right time. There is little to be gained from taking a back seat.

22nd – Let other people know exactly how you feel over conditions at your place of work. This also applies to housewives in the domestic situation. Partners will be cooperative and progress will be made.

23rd – Although your depression will have lifted, you now enter a period of being accident-prone. Be especially careful when handling hot and sharp objects or when operating complicated machinery.

24th – A day full of surprises, especially for those working from home. There will be a financial offer for some, promotional propositions for others; either way you should benefit from today's aspects.

25th – Keep yourself to yourself today when dealing with gossip-mongers. Certainly do not repeat anything you hear in confidence. This afternoon is the best time to deal with unfriendly neighbours.

26th – Do not sit around at home while others are off entertaining themselves. This is a day to get out there and enjoy yourself too and hang the expense! Let your hair down in no uncertain terms.

27th – Do not be too depressed should a long-standing relationship come to a close. Make the break a clean one and do not hang on to someone who wishes to let go.

28th – Changes are taking place around you over which you have no control, but do not worry as they should work out to your advantage. This evening is the best time for meeting up with relatives.

29th – You will be beset by financial problems, or rather a shortage of ready cash when you need it. Try to make sure that you have some reserve on hand to meet a specific bill that comes due for payment.

30th – A good day for meeting with superiors to discuss your career plans and ambitions. If you have any ideas to put forward, now is the time to present them – do so clearly and precisely.

31st – Try to get together with colleagues older than yourself if you need any advice or information about your work. Those at home will find that neighbours are willing to lend assistance if it is needed.

February

1st – Not the best day of the month for visiting relatives you have not seen for some time. Your presence will not be appreciated and they will be difficult to please. A stay-at-home day.

2nd – Try to be a little more understanding with the younger members of your family or friends. You are inclined to be too critical of their speech and actions today.

3rd – Not a good day for discussing business deals. A decision on which you are waiting will take a while to materialise and things will be left hanging fire for some time to come. You may have to shelve a favoured plan.

4th – Travel arrangements should be double-checked before setting out on a protracted trip of any description. Allow other people to make your bookings for you, since they are less likely to make mistakes.

5th – A good day for financial affairs. Ways of making extra cash will present themselves, but you must be quick to pick up on them. This afternoon is the best time for putting plans into action.

6th – There are some surprises in store for you on the domestic front and you may find them difficult to cope with. Try to remain flexible if your plans go astray this afternoon.

7th – A good day for getting to grips with career and personal problems. The advice of other people should be sought and acted upon. If you are lucky, you will get through the day unscathed.

8th – Friends make ideal companions this weekend and you should get together with them as often as you can. This evening is an excellent time for those who like a bit of a gamble.

9th – There is little to be gained in the way of entertainment within your own four walls. Get out and about with partners and loved ones and visit places you have not been to for some time.

10th – Those involved in litigation should find things going their way, as this is a good day for all legal activities. Aquarians professionally involved in the legal sphere will have an exciting and profitable day.

11th – Try to get the opinions of other people before embarking on a career change or pushing ahead with a difficult scheme. You could be making a mistake that is difficult to rectify later.

12th – Do not allow other people to interfere with your plans for this afternoon. Your judgement can be relied upon at this time. Financial matters should be dealt with now.

13th – Fatigue could be a problem today and it is unlikely that you will get through all you set yourself to do. Plan a relatively quiet schedule, but do not leave routine work uncompleted.

14th – Those in the home are advised against interfering with electrical appliances or carrying out do-it-yourself repairs. You could harm yourself or do more damage than good. Call in the professionals.

15th – There could be a set-back to something you are planning this weekend, but try to take it all in your stride. Although you feel disappointed, do not spoil the enjoyment of those close to you.

16th – A social event that you attend could produce that special someone you have been looking for, but do not make promises you are unable to keep. Those who are married should steer clear of the opposite sex.

17th – A good day for tying up business deals and for signing legally-binding documents. Important decisions made today will serve you in good stead in the future. Proceed with confidence.

18th – A business proposition that is put to you today appears to be sound, but check it out before committing yourself. There are some financial gains to be made through your own ingenuity.

19th – Midweek tiredness could lead to you making some elementary mistakes. Try to keep your mind on the job in hand and set aside some periods for rest and relaxation throughout the day.

20th – An excellent day for getting what you want from other people. This is the time to persuade superiors to make important decisions regarding your finances and your career. Favours will be granted.

21st – Regardless of your sex, you will find that men can be very helpful where finances and domestic life are concerned. Do not be too timid to ask for favours if they become necessary.

22nd – You may hear some rather disconcerting news from a family member, but you should not take this too seriously. A new circle of friends could be introduced to you this afternoon, so be on your best behaviour.

23rd – There is little to be gained from spending money in order to impress other people. Friends will be surprised at your apparent lack of financial restraint. Be a little more thrifty.

24th – You may hear that a recent plan of yours is in jeopardy. Do all you can to rescue it, as it has financial potential. This afternoon is the best time for seeking financial help from banks etc.

25th – Make the most of opportunities that come your way through friends. You may be invited into a scheme on a 'old pals' basis. Invest now and ask questions later.

26th – A business partnership could be crumbling at the edges and you will not know how to handle the situation. Seek legal advice if you think it necessary. Personal relationships are also under threat.

27th – Married Aquarians find partners confusing and difficult to handle; try to have sensible discussions, for something appears to be wrong. This evening is a good time for seeking advice and assistance.

28th – If there has been trouble brewing at your place of work, or on the domestic scene, it is likely to come to a head today. Do all you can to smooth troubled waters by being cool, calm and collected.

March

1st – Minor health problems will affect your day and you will find it difficult to concentrate because of headaches, etc. Plan a day free from tasks that require a degree of attention to detail.

2nd – Calls to relatives will pay off as far as goodwill goes. A financial proposition will be put forward by a friend, but you should question the motives involved.

3rd – Not a good day from the personal point of view. You are in danger of upsetting someone close to you by abusing their trust and loyalty. Do not take others for granted.

4th – Those attending business meetings and job interviews should make their opinions known and their presence felt. This is a day for positive action, thought and deed.

5th – New ways of making extra cash should be put into operation now, as there is the possibility that one of them could be a money-spinner. The ideas of those younger than yourself should be looked into carefully.

6th – Those working away from home will find it difficult to contact loved ones or the home workbase. Long-distance communications will suffer, so shelve important calls.

7th – Not a day on which to make hard and fast decisions that cannot be retracted later on. All important matters should be shelved for a few days. Younger people will be glad of some advice this evening.

8th – You could be taking it for granted that you are surrounded by goodwill where friends are concerned: it may be a different matter today. View everyone with a certain amount of suspicion.

9th – A good day for getting together with members of the family for a celebration of some description. Possibly there's a new addition to the clan.

10th – You could find a way of increasing your earning power and should take steps to further this end. Some surprising ideas come from colleagues, and you should consider them carefully.

11th – There is someone at your place of work who is trying to undermine your position. You need to do some detective work to find out who it is and what his or her motives are.

12th – A good day for all matters connected with the family and the domestic budget. Ways will be found of cutting down on your expenditure without putting loved ones' noses out of joint.

13th – Go all out to further a favoured plan or scheme today. Superiors will be willing to offer advice and enthusiasm, provided you appear enterprising and positive in your outlook.

14th – This is a day for letting your confidence out of the bag. Proceed with your plans and let no one interfere. Your judgement is good and you are well able to take care of yourself.

15th – A good weekend for mixing business with pleasure, although this will not go over at all well with family members or marriage partners. You will need to explain yourself with tact and diplomacy.

16th – The company of older people is favoured today, as you can gain from their experience and know-how. A hobby you have followed for some time could be put to good financial use.

17th – Do not allow other people to push you into the background – this is a time for you to outshine them all. If attending business meetings or conferences, make your opinions known and felt.

18th – A very good day for handling all legally binding contracts and agreements. Decisions can be made today with confidence. Rely on your intuition when dealing with strangers.

19th – You will gain through the misfortune of another, but in the nicest possible way. You will be able to take over where someone left off through inexperience.

20th – You may have to abandon a plan or scheme owing to lack of interest shown by other people. Do not let this put you off totally, as you should be able to reintroduce it at a later date.

21st – Do not spend too much time wandering in Memory Lane: what has been, has been. You could learn a thing or two from a younger member of the opposite sex in this direction.

22nd – A good day for getting out and about. Shopping sprees will be both remunerative in terms of bargains and good entertainment in terms of interesting happenings.

23rd – Try to spend the day as quietly as possible catching up on neglected personal tasks and minor jobs around the home. This is an excellent time for writing letters and making long-distance telephone calls.

24th – You will find it almost impossible to handle personal relationships, so you should keep yourself to yourself today. Those around you will behave in an eccentric manner.

25th – Someone with whom you have been at loggerheads for some time now offers to bury the hatchet – he or she will also be willing to make a few concessions to this end. Accept the hand of friendship graciously.

26th – You may be asked to organize a social event of some kind possibly connected with a club or association. Those professionally involved in sports will have a financially beneficial day.

27th – Give and take should be your motto for the day. Colleagues will be willing to assist you if you reciprocate. This evening is an ideal time to sort out the problems of a younger member of the family.

28th – Do not be too ready to jump down the throat of a marriage partner who is irritating you. Try to be a little more warm and understanding. It would appear that you are guilty of neglect.

29th – You will have so much on your hands today that weekend entertainment will have to take a back seat. Be prepared for others to accuse you of letting them down, but there is little you can do about it.

30th – A turbulent atmosphere within the home is probably of your own making. You will need to calm down a little and pour oil on the troubled waters. Personal relationships fare better this evening.

31st – The Monday-morning blues will seize you and you will be slow to get going, but once you do there will be no stopping you. Workmates will then begin to complain because they cannot keep up!

April

1st – Do not make any financial commitments this month, especially not today. Finances will need your urgent consideration. Try to find ways of increasing your income.

2nd – A good day for contacting superiors about your promotional prospects and the chances of a rise in salary. This afternoon is an excellent time for those out hunting bargains.

3rd – Do not allow other people to interfere with your schedule – they will cause you to make mistakes that will be difficult to rectify later on. Try to be more understanding with partners this evening.

4th – You will have great difficulty in completing the work you have already undertaken. Therefore do not be tempted to take on any more. Routine matters should be attended to first thing.

5th – A good weekend for getting out and about with friends. Try not to mix them with relatives as sparks could fly. This evening there are some problems to be sorted out with a youngster.

6th – Try to plan a quiet day in order to recharge your batteries for the coming week. You will have a trying time if you have invited relatives round. Catch up on personal matters.

7th – There is little to be gained from taking the lead today, especially if you are involved in discussion groups etc. Allow other people to voice their opinions while you look on.

8th – Do not overstep yourself financially, as you will be tempted to be extravagant. Spend only on essential items. This afternoon is the best time for contacting superiors.

9th – Have nothing to do with officials or bureaucrats – you can only lose out. Also avoid signing documents that are legally binding or that commit you to regular repayments.

10th – Fatigue could spoil your day, so you should plan a schedule that you can handle comfortably. There is little point in biting off more than you can chew just to impress others.

11th – Give as good as you get in all argumentative situations and do not allow others to shout you down. This is a time for making your presence and your opinions known.

12th – Changes in your social arrangements will lead to your upsetting someone close to you. This is unavoidable, and you will have to employ tact and diplomacy to extricate yourself from a ticklish situation.

13th – Do not allow friends to push you into doing something in which you would rather not be involved. This is a day when you should be doing your own thing. The evening should be spent in the company of family.

14th – A good day for getting what you want from other people, but do not be too pushy about it. Use some of your charm. Steer clear of get-rich-quick schemes – you will only lose money.

15th – As you will not be in the mood to have other people dictate to you, let them know this in no uncertain terms. People who are behaving in a very high-handed manner should be discouraged.

16th – Not the best day of the week for handling affairs that are connected with property, nor for doing jobs around the home. You will probably do more harm than good.

17th – Some people at work are trying to undermine your position; seek them out and have a few words with them. The motives of others will be difficult to understand.

18th – Those professionally connected with travel and transport will have an exciting and profitable day. Others will find that travel plans are foolproof and journeys trouble-free.

19th – Get out and about, as there is little enjoyment to be had within your own four walls today. Partners will be in an eccentric mood and have their own ideas as to how to entertain themselves.

20th – A good day for paying courtesy calls to relatives you have been ignoring for some time. You will have to be on your best behaviour this afternoon when you are introduced to an interesting stranger.

21st – If you wish to beautify your property and add to its value, now is the time to start making plans on this score. Do not put all your eggs in one basket – cheaper quotes for jobs can be found.

22nd – Try to track down elusive superiors who have been keeping you waiting for a decision over a career plan. You may feel like making some changes, but you should hold back for a while.

23rd – A good day for adding to your financial reserves. A new way of making extra cash will prove to be successful. The enterprising members of this sign will fare very well today.

24th – All joint financial commitments will come under review and you will need to make one or two cutbacks. In order not to upset those around you, consult them first.

25th – Changes that take place today will benefit you enormously in the future, especially those connected with your work. Do not make changes for change's sake however, as you will lose out financially.

26th – Be a little more resilient today and do not take things you hear about yourself too seriously. Make certain you are in full command of the facts before flying off the handle with a loved one.

27th – Not a good day for those connected with sporting activities or those who love the open-air life. Colds and chills are likely whilst on the move. Children will need your assistance and counsel this evening.

28th – Those making travel arrangements today are likely to run into several problems. These will make you late for an important meeting – try to leave on time.

29th – Be careful when dealing with tradespeople you do not know, as you could be short-changed or over-charged. Double-check your change after making purchases. A financial loss is likely.

30th – A good day for getting to grips with challenging tasks that you have been putting off for some time. You will find that a change from routine will do you a power of good.

May

1st – Minor health problems will have eased and you will be full of energy – quite able to get through the day and all you planned to do. This evening could be a hectic time, with relatives dropping in.

2nd – Relationships may go through another strained period. Try not to upset friends, as it will be difficult for you to patch things up later. Entertainment expenses will be high this evening.

3rd – A good weekend ahead provided you stick to whatever you have planned. Children, or older offspring, will be expecting you to keep promises you made some time ago – do not let them down.

4th – A good day for following a favoured hobby or pastime. There should be few interruptions and you can please yourself for most of the time. However, loved ones may be demanding this afternoon.

5th – Those who intend moving home this month have chosen a fortunate time for a change of scenery. Also, those involved with property professionally will find profits up and an enjoyable month ahead.

6th – Colleagues will be eccentric and difficult to handle, so you should go ahead with plans on your own. If you have a secret desire or ambition, now is the time to put it into operation.

7th – Occupy a back seat today and allow others to take the lead. You could glean some useful information just by keeping your eyes and ears open. Attend to the problems of family this evening.

8th – Your domestic scene may be a little chaotic today. Some will be moving home, some planning redecoration, and others will be trying to add to the value of existing property.

9th – If you have tradespeople working in your home, watch closely what they are doing – you may find that their work is sub-standard. You will have to take a firm line with people who are trying to take you for a ride.

10th – Again there could be some disorder at home, but you will be able to cope. A family emergency may take up much of your time, but you will be well satisfied with your performance.

11th – A good day for getting away from home for a few hours. You need a change of environment. This afternoon is an excellent time to visit friends or relatives.

12th – You may find that superior is out to cause trouble for you and you need to know his or her motives before you can take action. Do not let anybody belittle your capabilities or victimize you.

13th – Financially a good day. You should have one or two gains. They will not make your fortune, but they should ease the situation a little. Do not take loved ones for granted this evening.

14th – You may find that something you are organizing for the family or a loved one goes wrong and you have to retrace your steps. Do not be too depressed if things do not quite work out as planned.

15th – Work goes well and you should be making some progress.

Colleagues are helpful and will give advice and guidance if necessary. Children will need the help of parents this evening.

16th – There is little to be gained from following in the footsteps of others. Try to be as original as possible, therefore, especially in your concepts and ideas, thoughts and outlook.

17th – Romantic possibilities are somewhat confusing to you. What begins as a confrontation could end up as a liaison of hearts. This afternoon is a good time for mending broken friendships.

18th – Care should be taken when dealing with female members of your family, since their behaviour is likely to be erratic and hard to understand. Also, you may have difficulty in obtaining decisions from them.

19th – You could find yourself torn between your obligations to a work colleague and those to a friend. Make certain you let down neither. This is a bad day for all financial dealings, especially those of a joint nature.

20th – A fortunate day for all those connected with the property business. Good opportunities are around and it will be fairly easy for you to pick up on them. Domestic expenses will need your attention this evening.

21st – Those who are married will find partners cooperative and willing to go along with new plans for the home. Be sure to consult them whenever you decide to make any changes.

22nd – Do not become involved with a friend who has a get-rich-quick scheme that is on the wrong side of the law. You will be found out and all manner of trouble could ensue. Stay on the straight and narrow.

23rd – Care should be taken when dealing with strangers, also tradespeople with whom you are unfamiliar. Financial loss is likely in both areas due to your being too trusting.

24th – A good weekend for working in and around the home. All tasks carried out as a team will be successful. Enlist the help of friends if you need to complete something quickly.

25th – Those travelling today may find difficulty in getting to their destination on time, due to breakdowns and misdirection. Do not rely on your own transport or the directions of total strangers.

26th – As you are not in the mood for following other people, you would be wise to stick to your routine work and attempt nothing else. Ideally, you should be working alongside someone else for maximum success.

27th – It will be easier than you think to get what you want from superiors and those in positions of power and influence today. Just present your ideas, plans or demands in a positive and forthright manner.

28th – Not the day for dealing with legal and financial matters. There are losses indicated through confusion and carelessness. Watch where you put your portable valuables.

29th – It will be difficult for you to understand the behaviour of a work colleague who is normally friendly and helpful. Try to find out what the problem is, but use tact and diplomacy.

30th – A rather tiring day when nothing you do seems to go right, therefore you should attend only to matters of routine. Do not take on any extra responsibilities or challenging tasks.

31st – Those working in and around the home are warned against tampering with electrical equipment or appliances. You could injure yourself and also do more harm than good to the apparatus.

June

1st – Not a good day for visiting friends or relatives, so stay close to home and busy yourself there. Catch up on personal correspondence and a favourite hobby or pastime.

2nd – There should be little to cloud your day, but you must be prepared to handle the erratic behaviour of a loved one. You could be let down by a close friend this evening.

3rd – A good day for attending to the routine and tying up the loose ends of a business or personal matter. Financially this is not an excellent day, but at least there should be no losses of any magnitude.

4th – Call those people from whom you have been trying to get a decision for some time – you may just strike lucky. Superiors are easy to pin down. This evening is the ideal time for mixing business with pleasure.

5th – Those in the entertainment profession should receive a contract or a financial offer. Do not consider – sign, and ask questions later. This afternoon favours those in business on their own account.

6th – You should allow younger people to have their say today, as they have some good ideas for increasing work output and earning power. Try to be open-minded if their ideas seem a little way-out for you.

7th – A good day for getting out and about and mixing with other people. Some interesting strangers could become close friends, although their opinions may not quite match up with yours.

8th – Romance is likely from the most unexpected sources, possibly through an introduction made by a friend. Those who are married should not become jealous of the partner who flirts – it is quite harmless.

9th – Begin this week as you mean to carry on. Although you will not make much progess in a career matter, you will certainly enjoy yourself battling for what you believe is rightfully yours.

10th – A good day for attending meetings, discussion groups and conferences of any kind. You should make your opinions known, as today you will be positive and able to speak convincingly.

11th – A favourable time for attending to personal financial matters. You should be able to straighten out a problem that has been bothering you for some while. Allow other people to advise and guide you.

12th – Mid-week fatigue could be your problem, so do not plan a hectic schedule. Steer clear of jobs that require attention to detail or a lot of concentration. Care should be taken when handling tools.

13th – Make certain that other people know exactly what your objectives are and how you are going to achieve them; this may stop them from wasting your time today. Stick to doing all you set yourself to accomplish.

14th – Not the best weekend for getting your own way with other people. You will probably be running around after them for most of the time. Relatives will be quite demanding and they could upset you.

15th – Do not take younger people for granted today; they have some very good ideas for entertainment and for completing difficult tasks around the home. Allow them to have their say.

16th – You may find that you have to abandon a favoured scheme or plan owing to the lack of interest shown by other people, especially superiors. Shelve the idea, you will be able to use it another time.

17th – Catch up on business correspondence, as you are in danger of losing out through carelessness and lack of enterprise. This afternoon is the best time for dealing with financial matters.

18th – Give older people the benefit of the doubt this morning as you will need their help this afternoon. Be guided by what they have to say about your financial position – they are able to help.

19th – Stay cool today when a colleague makes a surprise announcement. It will probably affect your career plans – for the good. This afternoon is an excellent time for pushing ahead with plans generally.

20th – Do not allow other people to involve you in their schemes unless you have the time to participate. Financial assistance should not be given to anyone who asks for it – they are trying to take you for a ride.

21st Make the most of entertainment ideas suggested by friends, but take care that they do not come too expensive. If you think that you are going to spend more than you can afford, back out.

22nd – A good day for getting to grips with the problems of teenagers and other offspring. Advice that you give now will serve them in good stead for some time to come, but do not pressure them.

23rd – You could find it easy to rake in some cash. Contact those people who owe you money you loaned some time ago This afternoon is a bad time for putting joint finances at risk.

24th – Friends will have a great deal to say about your domestic arrangements, especially your financial situation. Do not listen to any advice they give, it will be totally unsound.

25th – Minor health problems will mar the rest of the month, with headaches and stomach upsets being the main causes. If you have any symptoms that concern you, contact a doctor or dentist.

26th – Those professionally involved with sport, speculation and children will have an excellent and most rewarding day. Financial advice given to you this morning should be acted upon this afternoon.

27th – There should be an upturn in your financial affairs today, possibly due to the arrival of a cheque or other payment for which you have been waiting. Try to save some money for future household expenses.

28th – Those travelling today will find their journey interesting and not a little eventful. Allow yourself plenty of time to reach your destination. Others will find their plans going awry for no apparent reason.

29th – Relatives and friends are likely to be irritable and difficult to please, therefore steer clear of them and spend your day as you wish. No matter what you organize for others, it will not go according to plan.

30th – Make colleagues aware of the fact that you are going all out to get what you want in the month ahead. This is an excellent time for you to make the necessary plans and contact the right people.

July

1st – Keep your mind on the job in hand, otherwise you are in danger of making mistakes that will be difficult to rectify later. Colleagues will be in a distracting frame of mind, so give them a wide berth.

2nd – Your domestic scene will have some bearing on what happens at work; try to keep yourself occupied. This afternoon is the best time for finishing off jobs that have been hanging fire for some while.

3rd – A good day for getting to grips with the problems of children and offspring. If you are professionally involved with children, then expect a day full of surprises – not all of them pleasant.

4th – Make the most of any favours that are granted to you today. Superiors and colleagues will be cooperative and helpful. You may have some trouble with a neighbour during the afternoon.

5th – Try to make plans for this weekend, otherwise you will find yourself wasting time wondering what to do. Friends are unlikely to call, so you will be left to your own devices.

6th – Relatives will be making some unexpected calls on your time and services today and you could be to-ing and fro-ing quite a bit. Give your time freely and do not complain.

7th – Financial matters will need your urgent attention today, possibly owing to the arrival of an unexpected bill. You will have to rob Peter to pay Paul. This evening is a good time for family get-togethers.

8th – Opportunities that come your way today will not be all they seem. Check them out before committing yourself. This is not a time to make hard and fast decisions. Tread warily.

9th – Partners are in restless mood and it will be all you can do to keep up with them. Make your feelings known in order to avoid argument and confrontation. Work colleagues will be more understanding.

10th – Minor health problems will affect your day. Depression is likely. Keep occupied and do not take youself too seriously. This evening should be spent in the company of light-hearted friends.

11th – You may need to practise some financial restraint in order to meet domestic liabilities. Do not be too extravagant and spend your money only on essential items.

12th – Entertainment expenses will come high, especially for Aquarians who are away from home at present. Those on holiday will be finding it difficult to make ends meet – you will have to economize.

13th – A good day for paying courtesy calls on relatives. Those younger than yourself will provide the best entertainment and you should direct your energies in that direction.

14th – Try to keep calm with work colleagues who are irritating and erratic in their behaviour. You will need to treat them with tact and diplomacy if you are to get through the day unscathed.

15th – Not a good day for meeting with friends or relatives. Stick to your own company. Those at work are advised to keep their heads down and get on with the job in hand

16th – You may be taking it for granted that those around you are helping your cause and your ambitions. You could be sadly mistaken, however. Keep you eyes open for someone who is trying to undermine your progress.

17th – Not a good day for attending business meetings or for signing legally binding contracts and agreements. Important decisions should be shelved until a more auspicious time.

18th – You may have to cancel a social arrangement made some time ago and this will not endear you to those concerned. Try to ease your way out of the situation rather than just cutting it dead.

19th – Make the most of a quiet time this weekend. Catch up on personal matters and minor jobs around the home. This afternoon will be the best time for making long-distance telephone calls.

20th – Marriage partners will be in a fun-loving mood and much enjoyment will be had in their company. This afternoon is the best time for talking about joint domestic plans for the future.

21st – A good day for tracking down elusive people, especially those who owe you cash or favours. Do not be timid about asking for what is rightfully yours. You may have to take a firm line with a neighbour.

22nd – Business contracts that have been hanging fire can now be concluded and signed with confidence. Do not allow other people to change your decisions. Your intuition is working well at present.

23rd – You could be faced with a minor upset in your career ambitions, possibly due to the intervention of a third party. Remain calm and make alternative plans.

24th – Cash will slip through your fingers today, so you are advised to be a little more thrifty than usual. Household expenditure will be high and you will need to rearrange your budget.

25th – Younger members of your work force could be giving you a difficult time, so you should have words with them and put them firmly in their place. This evening is a good time for home entertaining.

26th – All that you have organised this weekend could go out of the window unless you are careful. Make certain that you double-check everything and that people on whom you are relying are going to be in the right places.

27th – A day when your finances will again suffer a setback, but only a minor one. Try to keep your generous nature under control, as there are some people around who will willingly take everything you have.

28th – Career plans will receive a boost from a helpful female. Those out of work could receive assistance from an unexpected quarter. This afternoon is going to spring a surprise or two.

29th – You may find it very difficult to handle a personal relationship that has been running downhill for some time. It may be necessary for you to call a halt and break it off for good.

30th – You should handle all official business today. Bureaucrats and those in positions of power will be easily impressed. Those of you who are seeking a financial loan could strike lucky today.

31st – Another good day for finances. Bank managers are likely to smile upon your requests for an overdraft facility. Do not be afraid to ask for what you want – in all walks of your life.

August

1st – Depression will probably haunt you during the first few days of the month, so remember not to take yourself too seriously at this time. Today will bring some satisfaction over a career venture.

2nd – You should be on the lookout for ways to make your financial state a little safer. Friends and younger members of the family will have some bright ideas worth listening to.

3rd – Do not give way over an important family issue. Something that has been bothering you should be cleared up now, but you will need to take a very firm stand against opposition.

4th – Involvement with what others are doing could lead you to improve your income. The ideas of other people will work in well with whatever you have going at present. Neighbours could be irritable this afternoon.

5th – The single could find romance today and an interesting member of the opposite sex could become a permanent fixture.

Others will find romantic overtones throughout the day.

6th – Superiors will be willing to listen to good ideas which are well presented. Those at home will find the day rather boring, with only routine work to take care of – avoid making mistakes.

7th – Make the most of good opportunities that come your way. Your finances could be boosted if you take a chance or two. Those who like to gamble are advised to keep their stakes small.

8th – Not a good day for dealing with neighbours or tradespeople. If you have people working in your home, make certain they are doing their job exactly according to your wishes – mistakes are likely and will prove costly to rectify.

9th – You will find an extra touch of excitement throughout the day, and friends will provide some of this. Keep in touch with those you have not seen for some time – they have some good news to impart.

10th – Not the best day for calling on relatives, as their behaviour will leave much to be desired and you will not be made welcome. Try keeping yourself to yourself and remaining in your close family circle.

11th – There are some good career opportunities around at present and you should be taking advantage of them. Superiors will be willing to give you your head if you can impress them with your capabilities.

12th – Partners will be erratic and difficult to please, so try not to upset them in any way. You could find difficulty when dealing with people on a professional basis, so try to keep things friendly.

13th – You will be feeling a little nervy today, but do not let this spoil what you have planned. Stick to your schedule and do not allow other people to interfere. This evening is a good time for planning some relaxation.

14th – Avoid over-extravagance when spending money on the household. You could be taken for a ride by an unscrupulous tradesperson. Double-check change and purchases.

15th – Make certain that you attend to all business correspondence today, as you could lose out on an opportunity through carelessness. Work that needs attention to detail should be completed this morning.

16th – A good weekend for getting away from it all. If you are not already on holiday, try to get a couple of days' complete change of scenery – it will do you good and revitalize you for the coming week.

17th – Courtesy calls to relatives should be double-checked before setting out on your journey. Otherwise you are quite likely to find them out when you get there. This evening is a time for the romantics.

18th – Not a good day for tying up business deals or for signing contracts and agreements of a legally binding nature. Shelve all important decisions until a later date.

19th – Plans that were put into operation some time ago should now be showing signs of fruition. If this is not the case you will need to push them ahead just that much faster.

20th – Nieghbours will be willing to help out if you need their assistance today. However, do not accept favours that you know you will be unable to repay at a later date.

21st – A good day for sorting out a financial problem that has been bothering you for some time. You may need the help of a partner in order to get things back on an even keel.

22nd – All work that is carried out in conjunction with others will prove to be successful, as this is not a time to go it alone. Marriage partners will be cooperative should you wish to discuss your future plans.

23rd – Although you are accident-prone, you will have energy to spare, so attend to minor jobs around the home that have been left to hang fire. Take care when handling hot or sharp tools or appliances.

24th – You can call on the assistance of friends if you need them today; they will be willing to give their time freely. This afternoon is an excellent time for forming a professional partnership of some kind.

25th – Monday-morning blues could slow you down and make you careless in your work. Be certain that you do not make any elementary mistakes, as these will be difficult to rectify at a later date.

26th – A good day for dealing with the problems of children and offspring. If you are professionally involved, then you should have a satisfying and productive time.

27th – A relative could prove to be a stumbling block to a personal plan. You need to use tact and diplomacy in order to win him or her round to your way of thinking.

28th – Those searching for ways to make some extra cash could do worse than look to a hobby or pastime which could be turned to financial gain. This evening is an excellent time for mixing business with pleasure.

29th – Minor health problems will have subsided and you should be feeling more like your old self. This is a day to push ahead with plans and schemes. The afternoon is the best time for dealing with superiors.

30th – A good weekend for completing tasks around the home and for catching up on personal matters such as correspondence and telehone calls etc. Do not let younger people dictate to you this afternoon.

31st – Not the best day for dealing with family members. as their behaviour will be somewhat erractic and eccentric. You could also be feeling a little irritable – sparks could fly.

September

1st – This month begins on a low note as you are not feeling your best. Try to set aside some periods for rest and relaxation throughout the day and do not overdo your planned schedule.

2nd – A good day for seeking out people you need to contact with regard to a career matter. Elusive superiors can be pinned down, but you will need to be persistent and determined.

3rd – Those professionally involved with the arts, entertainment and creative pursuits will find today financially beneficial. Offers which come your way should be accepted at face value.

4th – There will be plenty of opportunities for you to earn extra cash and make your financial state a little healthier. Do not pass up opportunities just because they appear to be out of your field.

5th – A good day for attempting something new and taking on a fresh challenge. Routine work will run smoothly, but could prove to be boring. Those with extra responsibilities should put their best foot forward.

6th – A day to get out and see friends and relatives. There is little to be gained from sitting within your own four walls. This afternoon is an excellent time for those seeking romance.

7th – A family argument that suddenly flares up can be solved by conversation and discussion. Do not allow problems to multiply, but sort them out one at a time. A peaceful end to the day is in sight.

8th – The problems of a relative could prove to be the stumbling block of the day. Things that start out well will degenerate as the time progresses, since you will have to leave them to attend to your relation's affairs.

9th – Do not make any hard and fast decisions today, as you will have to go back on them at a later date. A good day, however, for making long-term plans – but not for setting them in motion.

10th – Midweek fatigue could let you down. Plan a quiet day and attend to routine work only. This afternoon is a good time for asking favours of colleagues and friends.

11th – Make the most of business discussions and interviews to put your points and opinions to other people. The unemployed will be best served by taking a positive attitude.

12th – Try to take a keener interest in what your work colleagues are up to, as you could learn something to your advantage. Keep your ears open when dealing with those younger than yourself.

13th – A good weekend for those involved with sports and sporting events. A minor celebration is likely. This afternoon is a time for getting together with the family and relatives.

14th – Work colleagues made ideal companions today and you could strike up a rapport that ends in a business partnership of some description. Try to attend to the problems of offspring this evening.

15th – What happens within the next day or two will be very important to you on both a career level and in your personal life. Decisions made at this time will be significant in the future.

16th – You may need to contact someone in the financial business to help you sort out a muddled official problem. This is not a day on which to make rash financial commitments.

17th – Steer clear of dealing with strangers. Those who are travelling will be misled and misdirected deliberately. Aquarians working from home will find the day running smoothly, with hardly any interruptions.

18th – The unemployed should make today a time of interviews and meetings – you could strike lucky just now. Others will find that the day is taken up by listening to the problems of other people.

19th – Not a good time for putting plans into operation, so shelve all important decisions until a later date. This afternoon is a good time for sorting out a domestic problem that has finances at its core.

20th – Make the most of help offered to you by friends. Work carried out in and around the home will benefit from many hands. This evening is an excellent time for seeking out inexpensive entertainment.

21st – You could be spending more time away from home today, so make certain that your method of transport is reliable. Delays and disappointments due to breakdowns could ruin an otherwise excellent day.

22nd – Changes that have taken place around you will now be working to your advantage. Career plans should be running smoothly and there is little to bother you on this score.

23rd – You may find it difficult to keep track of what is going on around you – there is just too much happening. Take a back seat and allow other people to lead whilst you follow.

24th – Confusion reigns again and you will be left wondering just what is going on. Steer clear of all complicated issues. This evening is a good time for mixing business with pleasure.

25th – You should be concentrating on your priorities and leaving everything else to one side. This is not a day for dealing with trivialities. All important decisions can be made with confidence.

26th – Be a little more optimistic in your outlook where a favoured plan or scheme is concerned. What starts out slowly will gather pace by the end of the day. Much good work can be achieved.

27th – Care should be taken when working in and around the home as minor accidents could occur, especially when working in high, exposed places. Those wishing to get out and about are advised to plan carefully.

28th – Not the best day of the month for family get-togethers. Relatives will be irritable and argumentative. A mild discussion could escalate into a full-scale family battle.

29th – The pace of the day will be set not by what you are doing, but by what others are achieving. You could be roped in to help out on a scheme or plan that will benefit you financially.

30th – Do not turn down the opportunity to work with other people, especially if the job is outside your field. The more challenges you accept today, the better off you will be.

October

1st – All plans should be running smoothly and you can proceed with confidence. Much good progress will be made by those working in import and export, and in the buying and selling fields.

2nd – A good day for attending to matters that are related to your domestic and personal life. A relationship that has been at rock bottom for some time can now be put on a firmer basis.

3rd – Not a day for the romantic. Partners will be irritable and difficult to please. You may have to cancel a social engagement because of the moods of a marriage partner or loved one.

4th – A good weekend for getting out and about. A change of scenery will do much to revitalize you. This afternoon is the best time for meeting with friends and relatives.

5th – You could add to your social prestige today by throwing a party or get-together at your own home. Invite people you know will be impressed by what you are trying to do. Mix business with pleasure.

6th – Career plans could be in for a setback and you will need to keep your wits about you at all times. The actions of colleagues will have a bearing on what happens throughout the day.

7th – Those at home are advised to call in the professionals if there are any breakdowns concerning electrical appliances. Do-it-yourself repairs are not advised – you will do more harm than good.

8th – Financial affairs could take a turn for the better, provided you are in tune with what is going on around you. There are some excellent opportunities for making financial progress.

9th – This is a good time for reminding other people of what they owe you, whether it be financial or moral obligations. You should be able to get whatever is due to you by being persevering and persistent.

10th – Do not allow other people to push you into the background today, but make your opinions heard. This is an excellent day for attending business meetings and for putting the finishing touches to outstanding deals.

11th – Try to be a little more enterprising today. A favoured pastime could be financially worth your while. Friends will be dropping by this afternoon and their advice will be invaluable.

12th – A good day for pleasing yourself. Do not allow other people to dictate your plans. Loved ones will be cooperative, but friends could be rather put out by your attitude.

13th – You could receive some very heartening news about a project or scheme you have under way. If you are in a business partnership, allow your partner to make all the important decisions.

14th – Check your mail this morning, as there could be something quite importrant for you to attend to. Do not shelve routine work today. Make certain that it is all up to date before you finish for the day.

15th – An ideal day for buying and selling. Those professionally involved in this type of work will have a very profitable time. Those working from home will find neighbours a constant source of irritation.

16th – Allow people younger than yourself to make some suggestions regarding your financial status. They could come up with some excellent ideas for improving things.

17th – You must find some outlet for your energies, otherwise you will become irritable and argumentative. Avoid confrontations with loved ones, as minor disagreements will blow up out of all proportion.

18th – If you are out and about this weekend, make certain you are well wrapped up against the elements, as there is a likelihood of colds and chills, especially when on the move.

19th – Relatives will be very irritable today, so you are advised to steer clear of their company. This afternoon is the best time for sorting out a domestic problem that has been hanging around for some while.

20th – Changes that are beginning to take place around you, especially at your place of work, will come out in your favour, so do not panic. This is an excellent day for sorting out financial matters.

21st – Be on your guard when dealing with officialdom in all its many guises. You could run into some opposition. This afternoon should be used for catching up on personal matters.

22nd – Do not take what other people say for granted – you may have to do some detective work of your own. Suggestions for making more cash should be treated with scepticism.

23rd – This is not the day for putting finances at risk. Those who like a gamble are advised to keep their cash in their pocket. Superiors will be difficult to pin down towards the latter part of the day.

24th – Try to keep yourself occupied during the day, otherwise boredom will set in. You may find it difficult to complete routine work, so set yourself an easy schedule.

25th – Cash spent on family entertainment will be wasted, as it will not come up to expectations. Disappointment in other areas of life should also be expected, especially where romance is concerned.

26th – Try to remain flexible today, as there is so much going on around you that you will have difficulty in deciding just what is best. Friends have some good ideas on entertainment this evening.

27th – Family matters will take precedence today and you will find that a long-standing problem is at last solved. Relatives should be able to give some good advice, if you are prepared to take it.

28th – It will be all to the good if you are stretched to full capacity today – the busier you are, the better you will like it. Colleagues may be passing their work on to you.

29th – Neighbours will be helpful and cooperative today, so you can call on them for favours if you need to do so. This afternoon is the best time for dealing with personal correspondence and other matters.

30th – Not a good day for sorting out the problems of younger people – they will not be willing to listen to your advice. Use tact and diplomacy when discussing their personal problems.

31st – You may have to take a firm line with those around you who are not meeting their obligations. This applies to family members and work colleagues. Do not be too relenting with offspring.

November

1st – Other people will be relying on you to provide the entertainment today, but do not be nervous about meeting their demands. You will find that they have utter confidence in your abilities.

2nd – A good day for family outings and get-togethers. Friends should be given a wide berth, as their ideas are too expensive for your taste. This afternoon is an excellent time for meeting relatives.

3rd – Do not be led into anything by those around you. They may be taking chances, but it is not good for you to follow suit. This evening is the best time for mixing business with pleasure.

4th – Do not deal with property affairs today. This is a bad time for all those wishing to buy or sell. Younger people will be trying to give you useless advice this afternoon – do not listen to them.

5th – If handling anything of an official or legal nature, do not attempt to go it alone. Get a professional in that particular field to deal with it for you. Children will be trying and demanding this afternoon.

6th – Financial matters will reach a head – it is likely that a bill has come in which requires immediate payment. Consult partners if you have any difficulty in meeting your financial obligations.

7th – A rather tiring day when you will need to set aside periods for rest and relaxation. Do not allow other people to push you beyond your capabilities. This evening is a time for recharging your batteries.

8th – Give as good as you get in family arguments. Do not allow others to override your opinions and ideas. This afternoon could be a rather traumatic time, but it will settle down before evening.

9th – Minor health problems will need your attention, so do not ignore any symptoms. Relatives who come calling today will be sympathetic and helpful. This evening should be spent resting.

10th – You could accomplish more than you expect today if you employ a bold and enterprising attitude. Other people will be willing to listen to your ideas if you are more positive in your approach.

11th – Financial matters could take a turn for the better now. There are some good opportunities around for you to earn some extra cash. Be prepared to put yourself out a little on behalf of someone else.

12th – Superiors will be willing to listen to your ideas, provided you can pin them down. This is one of the best days of the month for dealing with those in positions of power and influence.

13th – Make the most of challenges that come your way. Shelve routine work in favour of tasks that allow you to shine in the eyes of superiors. This afternoon is a good time for dealing with personal correspondence.

14th – It will be quite difficult for you to put a foot wrong today, so you can push ahead with confidence. Employ the help of other people whenever assistance is offered.

15th – Do your best to create a favourable impression if you are invited to a prestigious social event. You don't have to spend a fortune, just be yourself. Friends are likely to be supportive.

16th – Relatives will need careful handling today as they are in an irritable frame of mind. Use tact and diplomacy, especially with the older members of your family. Children are disobedient and demanding.

17th – A good day for the unemployed to attend interviews and write off for specific jobs. Lady Luck is on your side at present. Others will find that work runs smoothly, with little interruption.

18th – Some interesting news comes your way that will encourage you to greater efforts, in both your personal life and your career. Those in superior positions will be hearing of promotion.

19th – A good day for getting to grips with jobs that you have been putting off for some time. A particularly ticklish problem will now become easier to solve. An important day for all.

20th – A personal relationship in which you had been putting a lot of faith does not work out as planned. You may have to make a clean break from someone you considered to be very close.

21st – A good day for getting what you want from other people. Push your luck and you could surprise yourself with the results. Financial matters take a turn for the better.

22nd – A good weekend for all that is carried out on a team basis. Those connected with sports and sporting events will have a successful and profitable day.

23rd – A rather quiet day when you should catch up with all your domestic and personal affairs. Letter writing and telephone calls will be both pleasurable and time-consuming.

24th – Allow other people to take the limelight today, as some of it will rub off on to you. Be careful when dealing with superiors however – they are likely to be in an erratic mood.

25th – Avoid upsetting those around you. Explosive incidents are likely. This afternoon is the best time for tying up the loose ends of business deals and routine work that has been left for some while.

26th – A good day for those out hunting down bargains. Shopping sprees should be carried out away from your usual neighbourhood. However, take care with your personal possessions.

27th – Minor health symptoms should not be ignored. A visit to the doctor or dentist would not go amiss. This is an excellent day for attending to all your personal affairs.

28th – Make the most of opportunities that come your way. You may be put off by a work colleague when attempting something unusual. Those travelling today could find delays leading to disappointment.

29th – Not a good weekend for personal relationships, especially those of a romantic nature. Partners will be difficult to understand and arguments could ensue. Keep a low profile.

30th – Friends will have some ideas to discuss with you and you should make yourself available. Plans that are put to you today will be financially beneficial in the time to come.

December

1st – A good day for getting your own way with other people, especially on the domestic front. Partners will be easily convinced by your arguments. This evening is a time for family get-togethers and home entertaining.

2nd – Look at what other people are doing in order to give you some ideas on how to make extra cash. Those out doing early Christmas shopping will find that so-called bargains do not come up to scratch.

3rd – A good day for attending to business matters and career plans. Superiors should be made aware of your schemes. This afternoon is the best time for getting colleagues on your side.

4th – The events of the day will add to the personal enjoyment of your family and friends. Some news you receive from abroad this morning will have a great effect on your peace of mind.

5th – Minor health problems should be attended to as soon as any symptoms make themselves known. Do not ignore what your body is trying to tell you. This evening is a good time for resting and relaxing.

6th – Go all out for what you want from a personal relationship – this could be a make-or-break day. Romantic partners who have been somewhat cool in their relationship with you will need to be reminded of their obligations.

7th – Calls to relatives are advised, otherwise you will be getting complaints of neglect. You will find the experience a pleasure, as they are in good humour.

8th – Keep your thoughts on financial matters and how you can best overcome a sticky patch. If you have any bright ideas, make these known to other people – they will have the know-how to make them financially viable.

9th – A good day for getting to grips with a career problem. Superiors will be willing to give advice and assistance. This afternoon is a favourable time for signing documents and for making a financial commitment.

10th – Be careful with your personal possessions, since they are likely to be lost through your carelessness. If leaving your home unoccupied for any length of time, make certain that it is secure.

11th – An invitation to a social event is likely to come from a business associate or work colleague. Do your best to attend. Mixing business with pleasure could be financially beneficial.

12th – A good day for hunting down bargains and for getting in the Christmas goodies. This is not a time for handling business matters or anything related to your career.

13th – A fortunate weekend for those who like a bit of a gamble. If you keep your stakes within reason, you should end the day better off than when you started. This evening is good for home entertaining.

14th – A personal relationship will suffer at the hands of a third party. Try to remain calm and do not fly off the handle. The evening will find you in the company of relatives.

15th – Jobs that require attention to detail and any degree of concentration should be shelved for the time being. You are likely to make mistakes which will be difficult to correct later. Delegate wherever possible.

16th – Try to be a little more forgiving with those around you who cannot keep pace with you, or who do not come up to your expectations. Assistance rather than criticism should be extended.

17th – A financial problem you have been wrestling with can be easily sorted out with assistance from a friend. Accept any help that is offered in this direction. Children will need your guidance at some point today.

18th – If you employ staff then you can expect some ticklish problems, and you will have to sort them out quickly in order to avoid trouble. Those working from home will be subject to interruption and disappointment.

19th – A good day for attending to business matters and legal problems. You can sign contracts and agreements with confidence. This evening is the best time for planning your Christmas holidays.

20th – Parents will have to take a very firm line with offspring, as they are trying and disobedient. Discipline should be meted out. This afternoon is not the best time for family get-togethers or parties.

21st – Friends will be relying on you to provide entertainment, but you should discourage them. You have too much to do on your own domestic front; do not shelve any decisions in this direction.

22nd – Work colleagues will be in the mood to enjoy themselves, but you will not be of like mind. You could cause a few arguments by sticking to your guns – be a little more flexible and adaptable.

23rd – A good day for getting new schemes through to your superiors. All dealings with officials and officialdom generally will go well. Proceed with confidence. This evening is a bad time for seeing relatives.

24th – Invitations that come your way should be accepted, especially if they mean you can spend Christmas away from your own home. However, social events attended tonight will be fun and romance is likely for the single.

25th – HAPPY CHRISTMAS! Whether at home or away you should be able to enjoy yourself. Avoid becoming irritable with those around you. This evening could find you making new friends.

26th – Apart from the odd hangover, you should have an enjoyable day. Get out and about wherever possible for maximum enjoyment. Friends make ideal companions this evening.

27th – If out today, make certain that you are well wrapped-up against the elements as there is a danger of colds and chills. If staying at home, make certain that your companions are well looked after.

28th – A good day for resting and relaxing. Children will be a source of pleasure. There may be one or two trips taken down Memory Lane this afternoon, but do not dwell too long in the past.

29th – If back at work, make certain that colleagues are keeping pace with you, otherwise mistakes are likely. This afternoon is an excellent time for attending meetings and discussions.

30th – A romantic partnership will become more stimulating and you could even make a long-term commitment. Those who are married will find that partners are willing to listen to plans for the future.

31st – You will have some difficult decisions to make today, probably to do with your evening's entertainments. Avoid upsetting those closest to you. If attending parties it is time you let your hair down. HAPPY NEW YEAR!

The Moon and Your Moods

Our moods are clearly affected by the moon. After all, why on earth should such a well-balanced person as yourself be, on certain days, bad tempered, nervy, emotional, frigid and sentimental? Well, I'm afraid it is all down to the man in the moon. Prove it for yourself. Take a look at the moon table, then put it away for a month. In the meantime make notes of your moods, then rescue the table and you will notice a clear pattern of behaviour. You don't need an astrologer to work out for you that, during the month whilst you were making notes, the moon was in Scorpio when you were feeling depressed, in Cancer when you were feeling romantic, in Aries when you were bad tempered, etc. Your own individual pattern will be repeated each month; but do not be surprised if you are unaffected when the moon passes through, for example, Aries or Libra. Such a happening would merely indicate that these two signs are not particularly prominent on your birth chart.

Female readers would probably like to take a note of the fact that their menstrual cycle, if normal length, will begin when the moon is in the same sign each month. Why not have a try? You could find out a lot about yourself.

Moon Tables and Your Moods 1986

New and Full Moons 1986

January 10th new in ♑ Capricorn
26th full in ♌ Leo

February 9th new in ♒ Aquarius
24th full in ♍ Virgo

March 10th new in ♓ Pisces
26th full in ♎ Libra

April 9th new in ♈ Aries
24th full in ♎ Libra

May 8th new in ♉ Taurus
23rd full in ♐ Sagittarius

June 7th new in ♊ Gemini
22nd full in ♑ Capricorn

July 7th new in ♋ Cancer
21st full in ♒ Aquarius

August 5th new in ♌ Leo
19th full in ♒ Aquarius

September 4th new in ♍ Virgo
18th full in ♓ Pisces

October 3rd new in ♎ Libra
17th full in ♈ Aries

November 2nd new in ♏ Scorpio
16th full in ♉ Taurus

December 1st new in ♐ Sagittarius
16th full in ♊ Gemini

Key

♈ Aries   ♌ Leo   ♐ Sagittarius
♉ Taurus ♍ Virgo   ♑ Capricorn
♊ Gemini ♎ Libra   ♒ Aquarius
♋ Cancer ♏ Scorpio   ♓ Pisces

ADVERTISEMENT

YOUR BIRTH CHART by TERI KING
A BOOK OF LIFE

Simply fill in your details on the form below for an interpretation of your birth chart compiled by Teri King. Your birth chart will be supplied bound and gold lettered 'My Book of Life'. Send this form, together with your cheque or postal order for £12.50 (inc. p&p) payable to MERCURY CHARTS, to: TERI KING, c/o MERCURY CHARTS, Dept PBS, 20 Gerard Road, Barnes, London SW13 OPP. Allow 21 days for delivery.

Date of birth   Time of birth

Place of birth   Country of birth

Name

Address

Post code

A birth chart also makes an ideal present! Why not include, on a seperate sheet, the details of a friend or member of your family? Include £12.50 for each chart.

Julius Fast
Body Language £1.95

Every move you make reveals a secret . . . This important books adds a new dimension to human understanding. Julius Fast teaches how to penetrate the personal secrets of stangers, friends and lovers by interpreting their body movements – an how to make use of the power thus gained.

Francis Hitching
The World Atlas of Mysteries £6.95

From the origins of the universe and terrestrial life, through the unique development of man, to the secrets of ancient civilizations and bizarre phenomena in the sky and beyond – the enormous scope of this encyclopedia, its exhaustive research and copious illustrations (maps, photographs, diagrams) make it a unique and fascinating book. Francis Hitching, author of *Earth Magic*, is one of the world's leading authorities on the inexplicable and the unexplained.

'A book of absorbing interest to anyone who believes that there are more things in heaven and earth than science will recognize' DR KIT PEDLER, EVENING NEWS

Jean-Charles de Fontbrune
Nostradamus: Countdown to Apocalypse £2.50

He worked alone, a man versed in the secret writings, a historian of the future who generations have recognised as the greatest seer Europe has ever known. The rise of Napoleon, the Bolshevik revolution, two world wars, the sudden wealth of Arab power, the attempted assassination of a pope from Poland. And the chronology of the apocalypse. A Soviet invasion of Britain in the 1990s, the destruction of the House of Commons, nuclear holocaust in 1999, the year of the apocalypse . . .

Linda Goodman
Linda Goodman's Sun Signs £2.95

Have you ever wondered about yourself? What you are really like, whether you'll make a good wife, mother or lover, whether other people like you? Linda Goodman reveals the real you, your personality and character as the stars see you, in this remarkably lively and down-to-earth book.

Linda Goodman's Love Signs £3.95

A new approach to the human heart and personal relationships. A compulsively readable book exploring the tensions and harmony inherent in your associations with people born under the same sun sign as yourself, or under the other eleven signs. Also features: in-depth exploration of the seventy-eight sun sign patterns for both sexes; lists of famous people under your sign; explanations of the twelve mysteries of love.

Teri King
Love, Sex and Astrology £1.95

Revealing advice for would-be lovers. Spot your ideal partner; know the mating possibilities of the zodiac; find the strengths and weaknesses of your sign – through penetrating questionnaires. Teri King answers many questions on love, sex, careers and children with humour, wit and a deal of common sense.

'All quite irresistible' MANCHESTER EVENING NEWS

Leonard Cataldo and Robert Pelletier

Be Your Own Astrologer £3.95

Construct your own birth chart in under twenty minutes. Discover what the stars reveal . . . Two professional astrologers open up the world of astrology to everyone wanting to find the key to their unique personality. Armed just with your birthdate you can construct a simple profile. Or, to delve deeper, here's how to complete a complex chart, in fascinating detail.

Maurice Mességué
Health Secrets or Plants and Herbs £2.50

Man has been aware of the medical powers of plant life since the dawn of civilization. In this unique reference book, the famous herbalist Maurice Mességué describes the therapeutic properties of a hundred different species of plants and herbs, how to grow them and how to prepare the balms, lotions, infusions and ointments that will bring natural healing.

All these books are available at your local bookshop or newsagent, or can be ordered direct from the publisher. Indicate the number of copies required and fill in the form below

....

Name _____
(Block letters please)

Address _____

_____

Send to CS Department, Pan Books Ltd, PO Box 40, Basingstoke, Hants
Please enclose remittance to the value of the cover price plus:
35p for the first book plus 15p per copy for each additional book ordered to a maximum charge of £1.25 to cover postage and packing
Applicable only in the UK

While every effort is made to keep prices low, it is sometimes necessary to increase prices at short notice. Pan Books reserve the right to show on covers and charge new retail prices which may differ from those advertised in the text or elsewhere.